Praise for *Harald Harb's Essentials of Skiing* and PMTS Direct Parallel

"I've known and coached with Harald over the past twenty years. Harald is one of the few coaches who has studied and broken down all the components of skiing and coaching. His unique perspective on technique and equipment is based in science, and he has used it to develop the most logical complete system for training all levels of skiers and racers."

> —Crawford Pierce
> Program Director, Crested Butte Race Academy
> Former U.S. Ski Team Men's Technical Coach and
> U.S. Regional Racer Development Director

"Harald's extensive background in coaching and racing makes him a perfect candidate for developing great teaching and training methods. He also possesses an acute ability to communicate and express his ideas in a very effective manner. In this new book, Harald demonstrates his strong understanding of skiing by the breakout of fundamentals and foundations for skier development."

> —Thor Kallerud
> Partner, Thomas Weisel Partners
> Former U.S. Ski Team Head Men's Coach

"I would still be stemming my turns and struggling on hard snow and in the steeps had I not found PMTS, Harald's books and his instruction. There is no substitute for learning the true fundamentals of skiing which Harald details in his work. There is no faster way to expert skiing."

> —John Botti
> President, Botti Brown Asset Management
> Aspiring expert skier

"I can truly say that PMTS has changed my life. Because, since meeting Harald in 1999, I have moved my family to the mountains and now ski 80+ days a year (knock on wood). I truly am a 'junkie' and if there was a better choice for ski technique, coaching and equipment than PMTS and Harb Ski Systems, I'd be all over it. I'm happy to say my newborn son will be learning PMTS — that is, as soon as he's potty trained.
So watch out. If you follow PMTS you just might find yourself ripping lines you always dreamed about, moving to the mountains so you can ski more."

—Paul Kulas
Eagle, CO

"PMTS teaches you to become your own worst critic, which is a good thing, because most skiers don't know how to analyze their own skiing to realize that they may be skiing inefficiently."

—Sidney Tsui
Australia
Proud PMTS student of Winter '05

"I started skiing 3 years ago at age 48 and I am so grateful to Harald Harb for having this logical approach to developing a skier to their fullest.
I've been to many of his camps. My skiing friends that grew up on skis have been astounded at my rate of progress.
Thanks"

—John Mason

Harald Harb's
Essentials of
Skiing

Harald Harb's Essentials of Skiing

The words "Direct Parallel" are a registered trademark of Harb Ski Systems, Inc.
The words "Harb Skier Alignment System," "Primary Movements Teaching System," "Primary Movements," "PMTS," and "Harb Carver" are trademarks of Harb Ski Systems, Inc.

Hatherleigh Press
5-22 46th Avenue, Suite 200
Long Island City, NY 11101
Toll Free 1-800-528-2550
Visit our Web sites getfitnow.com and hatherleighpress.com

Disclaimer:

Before beginning any exercise and recreational skiing program, consult your physician. The author and the publisher disclaim any liability, personal or professional, resulting from the application or misapplication of the information in this publication. Skiing is an inherently dangerous sport. You should not depend solely on information gleaned from this book or any other for your skiing safety. This is not a substitute for personal instruction in skiing. Your use of this book indicates your assumption of the risk of skiing and is an acknowledgment of your own sole responsibility for your skiing safety.

Books are available for bulk purchase, special promotions and premiums. For more information on reselling and special purchase opportunities, please call us at 1-800-528-2550 and ask for the Special Sales Manager.

Library of Congress data available upon request.

ISBN: 978-1-57826-217-5

Photos, Photomontages, Illustrations, and Interior Layout by Diana Rogers
World Cup race photos provided by HEAD Sport AG, Wintersport Division
Cover Design by Deborah Miller, Allison Furrer

Photographed at Hintertux, Austria; Loveland Ski Area, Colorado; and Timberline Lodge in the Mt. Hood National Forest, Oregon.

The author appreciates the support of Head Tyrolia USA, for his sponsorship and for providing the World Cup race photos. The World Cup racers featured in the photos ski on Head Tyrolia products.

VISIT THE HARB SKI SYSTEMS WEB SITE
www.harbskisystems.com
NEW RELEASES • INSTRUCTION • CAMPS • EQUIPMENT INFORMATION

Printed in USA on acid-free paper

10 9 8 7 6 5 4 3

contents

A summer trip to Mt. Hood for our Race Camp. Combining our love for the outdoors with a ski camp means a camper stuffed to bursting with all our toys: fly fishing gear, bikes, tennis, and rock climbing. Where do we fit the Harb Carvers and the ski boots?

about the author

HARALD HARB IS PRESIDENT OF HARB SKI SYSTEMS. Born in Austria, he moved to Eastern Canada shortly thereafter. He followed his desire to become a skier from an early age, winning his first regional race in the Laurentian Mountains of Quebec at eight. Harald raced in his first World Cup race at 18 with the Canadian National Ski Team and later was the Overall Pro Ski Champion on the U.S. Eastern Regional Circuit. He then started to coach racers and became a director of racing programs. Harald's understanding of skiing movement developed through study of anatomy and kinesiology, as well as his coaching experience. Harald directed and coached programs that produced some of the USA's most successful National Team members and Olympic medalists. He has been a master coach in the USSCA organization since 1985. He was the program director in Alaska for Glacier Creek Academy, the program that developed Tommy Moe, who became an Olympic gold medalist.

After coaching for 20 years, Harald spent four years on the U.S. National Demonstration Team. He was a PSIA National Examiner and Trainer. Working with recreational skiers, he was convinced that current teaching systems needed improvement. Harald developed and established the Alignment Performance Center concept at Aspen and Telluride. Now he operates his own center. Harald created the Primary Movements Teaching System and the Harb Skier Alignment System so that skiers could learn movements and choose equipment to become experts quickly. He is the author of four books on skiing and skiing-related subjects. Over 100,000 lessons have been taught with his ski teaching system. PMTS Direct Parallel, as it is called, is the only teaching system currently in use that makes a clean break from the traditional wedge, wedge-christie progressions.

Harald also writes for magazines and several skiing Web sites. Harald Harb and Robert Hintermeister, Ph.D., co-author of the PMTS Instructor Manual, presented the PMTS Direct Parallel System and Harb Skier Alignment System to the 2nd International Congress of Skiing and Science in St. Christoph, Austria, in January, 2000. They presented Harb Carvers and further studies on PMTS Direct Parallel to the 3rd Congress in January, 2004, in Aspen, Colorado. The Association of PMTS Direct Parallel Instructors is a not-for-profit organization formed for the further education of ski instructors and promotion of Direct Parallel instruction worldwide. Harald is the Technical Director of the PMTS Instructor Association.

You can keep up to date with Harald and Harb Ski Systems on the Web site:

www.harbskisystems.com

My first love has always been all-mountain free-skiing.

note to racers

A WORD TO RACERS AND COACHES READING THIS BOOK. I am fortunate to have skied with Ingemar Stenmark. In my opinion, Stenmark is the greatest skier in World Cup history. His 84 victories are almost double those by any other skier.

Stenmark free skied perfectly. He practiced simple, fundamental movements in his free skiing, and it appeared that he used no effort. To the untrained eye, his free skiing looked unspectacular, because it was so steady. He could ski the entire "Liftline" run at Stratton, Vermont, with every known condition, from slippery ice to clumps of snow, without a single hesitation, wobble, or change in arc shape or speed. This doesn't sound like much until you try it on a run of over 1,500 vertical feet. I followed him and tried to match his turns.

Stenmark was to skiing what Roger Federer is to tennis. Federer has all the shots and he can make them under pressure. Stenmark had all the tools and he pulled off amazing recoveries in many races that he won, often not with good technique, but with desperation and athletic ability. The reason he could pull it out was because he skied with solid technique, with all the essentials built into his technique and trained into his skiing.

When Stenmark won runs by two seconds or more, he often had mistakes, not because he had errors in technique, but because he was going faster, much faster, than any other human had gone. He was testing the boundaries of skiing, body angles, carving, and edge hold. He was gliding, not holding an edge.

Racers need all the tools, but when used to perfection those tools produce edge hold and grip, not speed. This is fine for a recreational skier, but for racers there is a different objective:

*"Gliding with just enough edge hold, and edge hold without impeding
gliding, are the secrets to winning race runs."*

If your technique is solid and you know how to apply the essentials to
perfection, then you can apply them only as much as you need to create the
most speed. You will make mistakes and have to recover using this method,
but with solid essentials in your technique, you'll be within the range of recovery. Without the complete game, the mastery of all the essentials, you'll be skiing in the dark. You might go fast, but you'll never know when disaster is
going to hit, and you won't be able to recover. Without the essentials, you won't
have the tools to push your limits of speed. That's the limit that Stenmark found
and managed successfully.

*Kurt Engl, current Austrian World Cup skier, and Harald Harb, 1970s Canadian Ski Team.
Although equipment has changed dramatically in the past 36 years, the essentials of skiing have
not.*

introduction

THE GOAL OF THIS BOOK is to demonstrate and help you learn the most important individual components of skiing: the "Essentials." Many traditional ski tips are like window dressing: they might refine or tweak your skiing. Without the essentials of this book firmly in your command, other tips are like trying to put a glossy paint job on a rusty car. The essentials described in this book are categories of movement that are universally applicable and beneficial: whatever your current level, working on the essentials will accelerate your progress, giving you command of any terrain. Working on the essentials will improve your balance and let you strive for higher standards of balance. Practicing the exercises in the book will raise the quality of your movements, tangibly improving your technique, and giving you the confidence to approach all terrain that you aspire to ski.

The four ski books I have written so far have been based on my experiences in skiing: in racing, as a former international racer and as a coach; as an instructor; and as a trainer of other instructors. The knowledge I gained through my coaching career is extensive, gained during 35 years of training, educating, and practical involvement with world-class athletes, coaches, as well as weekend athletes. My participation as a competitor and coach in sports other than skiing — cycling, tennis, and soccer — has also been educational and has helped me in my innovation of skiing technique, technology, and teaching.

The need for simplification in sports techniques and instruction became evident to me early in my coaching career. Not only did I feel there was a need for more accurate and concise information, but also for better delivery of information in order to ease assimilation, understanding, and implementation.

My answer to these needs was to develop the Primary Movements Teaching System ("PMTS"), and then to create instructional materials — books and videos — that would bring this technique directly to skiers in order to make their skiing and learning easier. Let's take a quick look at my other publications to see where this new book, *Harald Harb's Essentials of Skiing*, fits in.

Expert Skier 1

My first book, *Anyone Can Be an Expert Skier 1*, is aimed toward skiers that I thought would be most interested in working on their technique: novice, intermediate, and advanced skiers who had learned traditional technique, but were not able to improve or reach their desired perfor-

mance level. The book presents a linear approach to learning the movements of PMTS technique with sequences of exercises that isolate the critical movements and that build upon each other to integrate those movements into skiing.

The *Anyone Can Be an Expert Skier 1* book introduced a revolutionary concept: a simple sequence of easy-to-perform movements lets the skier link the end of one arc directly to the beginning of another, developing an almost instant parallel turn. I named this sequence the "Phantom Move."

In traditional ski instruction, the act of connecting one arc to the next requires years of training to understand, includes many complicated and extraneous details, and often takes years to learn to perform with the skis parallel. The transition between turns involves releasing and then engaging both skis while the body moves to the other side of the skis for the next turn. The act of transition, required each time we want to get into a new turn and gain control on the slopes, requires the biggest change in body position in the shortest time. The simple movements that are critical to successful turn transitions are tipping or tilting the feet. Unfortunately, these movements have been neglected by traditional instruction to the detriment of most skiers. In PMTS technique, tipping movements beginning at the feet come before all other movements, and are first and primary in establishing a set of fundamentals that will speed skiing progress.

Another concept introduced in *Anyone Can Be an Expert Skier 1* was the separation of the roles of the feet: the outside foot in an arc is the stance foot, on which you maintain balance, while the inside foot and leg perform the tipping and flexing that control the arc of the turn. This was at odds with traditional instruction, in which the outside ski is weighted *and* turned, while the inside ski comes along for the ride. The Phantom Move, developed in *Anyone Can Be an Expert Skier 1,* is the combination of balance transfer and free-foot tipping that produces an easy parallel transition. It is often described as the "lift and tilt" move.

The concept of pulling the free foot back in order to manage fore/aft balance was also introduced in *Anyone Can Be an Expert Skier 1.* The book contains an extensive section on equipment and alignment, and how it pertains to your skiing performance and progress.

Instructor Manual

My second book is the *PMTS Direct Parallel Instructor Manual*, written specifically for instructors who would like to teach PMTS technique. While my first book, written for skiers, presumed that readers already skied at some level using traditional technique, the manual teaches Direct Parallel technique. By applying the movements of PMTS technique to first-time skiers, those skiers could avoid learning the wedge/snowplow, and thus not encounter the same learning and performance difficulties as skiers who learn traditional technique.

The manual still covers the techniques needed for working with skiers who learned traditional technique, since they represent the

Dynamic skiing is for all ages — I'm 58 this year.

vast majority of skiers on the hill. Lucky are the new skiers who find a PMTS Direct Parallel ski school! Instructors who become accredited in PMTS Direct Parallel must demonstrate proficiency at teaching both streams of skiers: novices who learn Direct Parallel, and those who come from a traditional-technique background.

Expert Skier 2

My third book, *Anyone Can Be an Expert Skier 2*, is the natural continuation of the first book. With the progress that came through use of the first book, skiers would be ready to build upon their new technique with greater carving angles, carved short turns, control on steeps, and adventures farther from the groomed slopes.

The *Anyone Can Be an Expert Skier 2* book is presented in two sections. The first section takes the same primary movements that were previously introduced and offers a linear exercise approach to integrate these movements into short turns. Once a reader has mastered short turns on steeper terrain with a solid pole plant, the second section of the book applies this "bulletproof short turn" in different terrain, to work on changes in technique that are specific to certain conditions (such as exaggerated flexing of both legs in deep moguls).

Essentials

The question then arises: why the need for this new book, *Harald Harb's Essentials of Skiing*? The answer is simple: With a fresh look and an innovative approach, it welcomes new enthusiasts and keeps my previous readers engaged in the process of improving their skiing. This new book offers a different approach to learning with the Primary Movements Teaching System.

As its name suggests, the Primary Movements Teaching System is based on the *movements* that create expert skiing, teaching the same movements to all levels of skiers so that they progress most rapidly. My three previous books were organized in a linear fashion, where the tasks presented incorporated one or more of the Primary Movements, and the order of the tasks developed the reader's movement capability as they progressed through the book. This book is organized around the key *movements* of skiing. Each section of the book takes one of those movements — an essential — and develops that movement through a series of exercises.

Why Another Book on Skiing?

Let's not forget that skiers go to ski resorts to ski, golfers go to courses to play, and tennis players go to the court to play games. We know that skiing is fun, entertaining, and provides an outdoor experience that's hard to duplicate — this is what most skiers want out of skiing.

Don't get me wrong: I'd rather see a skier skiing downhill — even with marginal technique, not really getting much from their skis — rather than sitting in front of a TV, eating chips, and drinking beer. However, in order to access the fun of skiing, one requires certain abilities. To truly have a great skiing experience generally requires more than regular ski instruction.

Many skiers don't see the need for ski instruction or for a well-planned instruction program. They just ski and enjoy it, without regard for technique. There are other skiers, though, who are devoted to improvement, who seek a higher performance level, and who know that their enjoyment of skiing will increase along with their progress. My books are written for these skiers, who are searching for the information that will bring them the most benefit in the shortest time. My books are for skiers who want to carve the groomed slopes with poise and ease, to ski the whole mountain, perhaps to challenge themselves on bumps, steeps, and powder, and for those who want to ski late into their maturing years. If you are one of these skiers dedicated to learning, it is my hope that this new book will bring you the progress you seek.

Form comes from function. PMTS technique offers recreational skiers the fastest road to success.

Exercises Developed from Teaching Our Students

After coaching at almost all of our camps in the four years since writing *Anyone Can Be an Expert Skier 2*, I have seen the needs of our many dedicated students. These students are the inspiration for this book. Exercises I used or developed for these skiers are the basis for this book. I found that many of my students, at the end of a camp or lesson, would ask me to write out all the exercises we worked on. The exercises practice specific movements of the body that are needed to ski well. With its assembly of exercises grouped according to movement, *Harald Harb's Essentials of Skiing* explains, demonstrates, and helps you learn the aspects of skiing that are necessary for truly expert performance.

For each exercise in this book, I've described the benefits of (or reason for) the exercises. I describe common scenarios of skiing difficulties so that you can identify the exercises or movements that will benefit you the most.

Harald Harb's Essentials of Skiing — *innovative approaches for novices through experts.*

How to Use This Book

I include this section in my new book because I have had seven years to evaluate the impact of *Anyone Can Be an Expert Skier 1*, and four years for *Anyone Can Be an Expert Skier 2*. Most of the skiers who come to Harb Ski Camps have read one or both books, or have watched one or both videos. This gives me first-hand information to judge the effectiveness of the publications. I listen to the skiers tell me how they practice what they read or watched, and I watch them ski. Most of these skiers, and others who communicated by phone or e-mail, tell me that the *Expert Skier* books have made a huge difference in their skiing. I don't have the luxury of making the comparison of how they skied before they started using the Primary Movements Teaching System. What I can evaluate is how, at their present level, they use and perform the movements of PMTS.

These skiers are eager to learn and improve, and they are always looking for a better methodology — specifically, a methodology that solidifies their skiing and gets proven results. It is for this reason that most skiers bought my books and videos.

It is easy to see that skiers are fascinated by the Primary Movements Teaching System, and especially by the Phantom Move. They practice the Phantom Move diligently, following the instructions in the books or videos, and perform it with varying degrees of success. In the *Anyone Can Be an Expert Skier 2* book and DVD I clarified the Phantom Move, adding more information, since many skiers were only incorporating part of the Phantom Move into their skiing, thus not achieving the full benefit.

Over the last four years, I have seen common themes among skiers who have self-taught from the books. Since my intent in writing books is to help skiers improve, this book must not only present exercises, but also guide the reader in getting the most out of the book.

To make sure you are on the right track and get maximum value from *Harald Harb's Essentials of Skiing* here are some suggestions:

1. Read the book from beginning to end before any on-snow practice.
2. Evaluate your understanding of ski technique relative to the overview of the essentials.
3. Practice and use the movements that you are capable of before you move to higher, more difficult levels of movement.
4. Be willing to be "uncomfortable" during the learning process. Being comfortable often means that you are performing habitual movements, whereas the first few times you perform a new movement, it might not feel good, comfortable, or natural, simply because it's not your habit to perform it.
5. Verify your performance — just because you perform an exercise doesn't mean you have done it correctly. There are several methods of verification: having a friend or coach watch; video footage (compare with the book's photos); external cues (as demonstrated in the book); and ski track analysis.

Harald verifies performance with video at a Harb Ski Camp. Concentration and focus are high when skiers understand their movements and opportunities for success.

Ultimately, you'll make the most progress in your skiing if you can identify the component that is weakest and then work on it. Because this book is arranged by essentials, you can focus on one essential that you have determined to be your weakest, and know that all the exercises for that essential will benefit you. How to make this determination? Perform some of the early exercises for each essential, verify your performance as mentioned above, and pick the one where you have the most difficulty, or where you seem furthest from the performance demonstrated in the photos. If you have trouble knowing what to work on, consider coming to a Harb Ski Camp or taking a lesson with a PMTS Accredited ski instructor. The personalization of movement and instruction will speed your learning.

Read on — I wish you good progress in your skiing!

*"Quality skiing is a matter of
relaxing at the right time,
not of forcing turns."*

CHAPTER 1

The Essentials

THE GOAL OF THIS BOOK is to describe, demonstrate, and help you learn the "essentials" — those movements that are the basis for solid ski technique. Practiced at any level, the essentials will speed your progress and provide more success on any terrain.

The exercises that develop each essential have been selected from the many that we use in our camps and lessons. We have used them with many skiers with good success. After years of giving camps for all levels of skiers, we have the advantage of seeing where novice and intermediate skiers go wrong, where the technique they are using heads them down a dead-end path. With ineffective, inefficient technique, these skiers are using too much effort and getting too little reward. Sure, with persistence and effort they may progress to become advanced intermediates, but the bottom line is they're never going to become really good skiers simply because they aren't using the movements that create good skiing.

Some readers might be thinking that they'd be happy to reach advanced intermediate status by any method. If you knew that your method would require more effort, cause more stress on your joints, and ultimately stop yielding progress, would you want to choose that route? I didn't think so. Instead, let's get started on the path to efficient, effective technique. From our camps, we have the benefit of seeing which exercises are the most effective at helping skiers learn the new technique, in the shortest time.

The best skiers — World Cup racers, developing racers, experts (be selective when observing; not all skiers on black diamond terrain are experts) — use different technique than what is typically observed on the slopes, and it's certainly different from the dead-end technique of many intermediates. In my 35 years of coaching and observing, I have determined the movements that are used by these top skiers.

The essentials presented in this book are those expert movements, presented in numerous exercises so that you can learn them. If prac-

ticed and integrated into your skiing, these movements will take your skiing to a new and rewarding level. They are simple movements that can be practiced on your own throughout the season, or they can be learned in a five-day camp. It's never too late to learn the essentials. Even if you are a seasoned skier with years of habits, through diligent practice and verification you can learn the new technique. This book explores each essential, developing the foundation of skiing that will never let you down.

Figure 1-1. *The Sample Turn — stretched.*

The Sample Turn — A Turn for All Skiers

The "Sample Turn" is used to demonstrate all of the essentials. It is a normal, free-skiing turn, on intermediate terrain, within the capabilities of most skiers. The photomontage of the sample turn starts in the middle of an arc to the right,

continues through transition, then into the beginning and middle of the next arc (toward the left). By using the same turn to demonstrate all of the essentials, you can see how they work together.

It is important to mention that this montage is "stretched" — the individual frames have been moved apart in order to create a clear, non-overlapping image, but the dynamics of the ski arc are still portrayed. In reality, this turn takes much less space. The true montage is presented here for comparison. Though the stretched version of the Sample Turn will be used throughout the book, you can always refer back to this image for the true spatial representation of the turn.

Figure 1-2. *The Sample Turn — actual positions of individual frames.*

The Essentials

The essentials of skiing are

- *Tipping*
- *Flexing and extending*
- *Counteracting*
- *Counterbalancing*
- *Combining counteracting and counterbalancing with pole use*
- *Maintaining fore/aft balance*

Each essential will be described and demonstrated in its own section.

Tipping

I begin *Harald Harb's Essentials of Skiing* with tipping. Tipping is the most important of the essentials for two reasons. First, tipping actions of the feet and legs activate the kinetic chain, encouraging the rest of the body to maintain balance. Second, tipping is the movement that happens closest to the snow, and the snow is the only solid surface with which we interact in skiing. Establishing a strong relationship to the base of support — that is, contact between feet, boots, skis, and snow — should come first in your skiing. Thus tipping is the foundation for edge grip, edge change, ski performance, balance, and terrain absorption.

TIPPING ENCOMPASSES MORE THAN MOVEMENTS OF EDGE CHANGE

Let me repeat that tipping movements are the foundation of skiing. Proper tipping allows and directly enables necessary components of expert skiing, like edge hold.

> "If you know how to achieve edge grip, you don't need to look for it; if you don't know how to achieve it, finding grip becomes an overriding compulsion."

Unfortunately, the harder you try to find it, the less likely it is that you achieve it. This theme is consistent in many sports. The harder you try to hit the golf ball, the less likely it is that you hit a good, long shot. The harder you hit the ping-pong ball, the less likely it is to hit the other side of the table.

In skiing, when your tipping movements are not well developed and you're likely to be looking too hard for grip, here are some common results:

1. As more effort is applied to make the edges dig in to get grip, the less effectively the skis grip.
2. As you put more effort into turning, your arcs and carving disintegrate.
3. The harder you push against the snow, the more your balance goes out of control.

There is a way to move, to tip your skis, that grants access to edge grip, arcing skis, and balance. This book will guide you to this way of tipping and the methods to obtain it will be very different from the traditional understanding of skiing.

Take a look at the Sample Turn, Figure 1-1, and answer these questions:

- In how many frames are the skis on edge, with the bases lifted off the snow?
- In how many frames are the ski bases flat on the snow?

Of nine frames, there is only one in which the skis are flat. In all the others, the skis are on edge.

Remember that this montage has been stretched — there is more space between the frames in the image than in reality. The photos for this image were shot at 7.5 frames per second. This means that the period or distance over which the skis are actually flat on the snow is less than one ski length! The only way that this can be achieved is to perform the transition without hesitation. There can be no hesitation in the release. The momentum from the release must take the body and skis through the edge change. One can see from this image that in skiing at the expert level, one should be standing on the ski edges — holding the skis tilted at an angle to the snow — almost the entire time through a series of linked arcs.

Back to the Sample Turn. In which frames is there an effort to increase the tipping angle? In which frames is there an effort to decrease the tipping angle? Are there frames where the tipping angle is sufficient, and thus maintained at that angle into the next frame?

Since I am the skier in this montage, I can convey to you in which frames I increase tipping and in which frames I decrease the tipping. Here again is the sample turn, this time spread over two pages.

From Frames 3 to 6, I am already focusing on tipping my skis to the *new* edges. Most skiers don't think about getting to the new edges until Frame 7 or 8. If instead you think about and begin tipping toward the new edges starting at Frame 3, you will create momentum in tipping toward those new edges. This momentum makes it easier to change edges and achieve early edge angles. If you delay your tipping toward the new edges until Frame 7 or 8, you won't have the momentum of tipping built up to help with the transition, and you typically have to substitute physical effort or strength in order to switch edges. Similarly, if you pause or otherwise interrupt your tipping efforts toward the *new* edges, you won't link one arc to the next. Any hesitation in this tipping gener-

Figure 1-3. *Tipping demonstrated in the Sample Turn (left and right; stretched).*

Frame 1. *Increase tipping.*

Frame 2. *Increase tipping.*

Frame 3. *Maintain that angle.*

Frame 4. *Decrease tipping (releasing).*

Frame 5. *Decrease tipping through flat.*

Frame 6. *Increase tipping to new edges.*

Frame 7. *Increase tipping.*

Frame 8. *Increase tipping.*

Frame 9. *Increase tipping.*

ally leads to a skier trying to *turn* the skis at the moment of transition — aiming them in the new direction rather than tilting them to the new edges. With continuous tipping toward the new edges from Frame 3 you'll develop what I call the "High-C" portion of the turn — balance over the arcing ski in the upper half of the turn. With

hesitation, you'll feel the urge to turn the skis, ensuring no arc and no ski performance in the beginning of the new turn. This hesitation, and the need to add "something" to get the turn started, is evidenced by upward movements of the body, extension of the leg, pushing off the new edge, and/or body rotation.

TIPPING IS NOT TURNING

I need to make an important clarification in terminology, between *tipping* and *turning* the skis. *Tipping* the skis makes them roll on or off edge, or to a greater or lesser edge angle. During this process, the skis do not point in a new direction; they continue to point in the same direction throughout the tipping. *Turning* the skis does not change their edge angles; it changes the direction that they point. If you were to draw a giant clock face on the snow, and stand in the center of that clock with your skis pointing toward 12 o'clock, you could *tip* your skis back and forth and they would continue to point at the 12. If you were to *turn* the skis, they might point at 10 or 11, or 1 or 2 — they would not continue to point at 12.

Traditional ski technique includes *turning* the skis — a deliberate effort to make them point in a new direction — as part of each turn. With modern equipment, *turning* the skis is unnecessary. Instead, we need only to tip the skis on edge and balance on them as their flex and sidecut makes them travel in an arc across the snow.

When we tip to the other edges, the skis arc in the other direction. Whether we call this serpentine path that the skis make "linked arcs" or "linked turns," remember that a *turn* is a result that the skis make, not an effort that we must perform.

Turning the skis will reduce their grip, make you battle for balance and control, and reduce your ability to use momentum to get from one turn to the next, so you'll need more effort to start each turn. *Tipping* is a critical component of PMTS technique because it is the movement that lets the skis do more work, and the skier do less work. It lets you achieve early grip, and lets you use momentum to link arcs — both hallmarks of expert skiing.

Chapter 2, Tipping, will give you an opportunity to evaluate your ability to tip and to balance while tipping. Many of the exercises look easy, and you might be tempted to skip over them. Please avoid this temptation — practicing even the most basic tipping exercises is fundamental to expert skiing.

Figure 1-4. *All the essentials are needed to produce a quality transition between turns.*

Flexing and Extending

Flexing the leg — shortening or bending the leg — is a movement not commonly used by skiers. Extending the leg — lengthening or straightening — is often used to move the torso vertically upward. In the Primary Movements Teaching System, flexion of the leg is a fundamental movement. Flexing (bending) the old stance leg (downhill or outside in a turn) is used along with tipping to start the release, enabling the body's momentum in one arc to assist in transition to the next. Continued flexing of this leg, now the inside, helps the body to move inside the arc of the skis, producing early and high body angles for the turn. Extending (straightening) the outside leg *after transition* contributes to achieving these early and high angles. In PMTS technique, extending the leg is *not* used to create the turn transition. In fact, an upward extension of the leg(s) to create a turn transition delays or interferes with building edge angle for the upcoming turn. Through the exercises in Chapter 3, Flexing and Extending, you

will learn the essential of flexing and extending — how, when, and where to bend and straighten the legs.

Another concept that will be explored is the relationship between the inside and outside leg. In order to develop deep edge angles, one needs to know how to flex the inside leg deeply (bend it a lot) while keeping the outside leg extended (almost straight). We often refer to this relationship between the legs as "long leg/short leg."

One misunderstanding regarding flexing (bending) held by many skiers and instructors is that flexing is muscle intensive and tiring. Yes, improperly-timed flexion can tire the legs. But with proper timing relative to the turn arc, flexion requires very little effort. If you are making an arc where your body is angled inside the turn, then the momentum of the turn is already trying to squeeze you against your outside leg. You have to have some resistance in your outside leg to prevent being squeezed like an ac-

cordion. In order to flex, then, all you have to do is relax and diminish your resistance. You don't have to increase your effort to flex or bend the outside leg, merely decrease it! Once you learn to coordinate this relaxing or flexing with the decrease in tipping angle described above in the section on tipping, you'll be linking arcs with early and high edge angles.

Why do I keep pushing for high edge angles? If you are an intermediate skier, high edge angles may look scary or intimidating. However, when your skis are tipped to a high

edge angle, they provide secure, confidence-inspiring grip, and they support balance.

Let's look at the Sample Turn photomontage to observe two occurrences:
1. Where flexing (bending) the old stance leg reduces edge angles and starts the release.
2. Where flexion (bending) of the inside leg and extension (straightening) of the outside leg increase edging and body angles for the arc.

Figure 1-5. *Flexing and extending demonstrated in the Sample Turn (left and right; stretched).*

Frame 1. *The stance leg (outside) is almost fully extended and the free-foot (inside) leg is more bent.*

Frame 2. *Maintain Frame 1.*

Frame 3. *Increase flexing (bending) the stance leg.*

Frame 4. *Increase flexion of stance leg until is as flexed (bent) as the free-foot (inside) leg.*

Frame 5. *Both legs are equally bent. Lighten the new inside ski.*

Frame 6. *Flexing the inside leg; extending the outside leg ONLY to maintain contact with snow.*

Frame 7. *Inside leg is light and continues to bend; the outside leg lengthens to maintain snow contact — not to push or move your body by extending against snow.*

Frame 8. *Same as Frame 7.*

Frame 9. *Inside leg is flexed; outside leg is extended.*

Counterbalancing

Counterbalancing is simply side-to-side tilting of the upper body at the waist or belt line. Coordinating this movement of the torso with tipping will give you confidence to be on edge, in balance, at the top, High-C part of each arc. It's important to note that tipping (Essential #1) is the first or primary quantity; counterbalancing should be performed in proportion to tipping, to complement the tipping. If the tipping actions starting at the feet diminish or cease, then no amount of counterbalancing — tilting movements of the torso — is going to make up for the loss. Through Chapter 4, Counterbalancing, you'll learn how to counterbalance and how to coordinate it with your tipping.

Why do we call it counterbalancing? Because the movement of the torso is opposite the direction of tipping. Imagine that you are tipping your skis to the right, starting the tipping action with your feet. Your legs will follow and start leaning toward the right. If you also lean the torso toward the right (leaning your right shoulder toward the ground on your right side), one of two things will happen: you will tend to lose your balance as though to fall toward the right, or you will have to flatten the skis (reduce their tipping angle) in order not to fall.

You can think of counterbalancing acting in two ways, static and dynamic. In the static sense, tip your feet as far to the right as you can, and balance there for 5 seconds. During that period, you'll have to have some leftward tilt of the torso to hold that position. In the dynamic sense, tipping your feet toward the right creates momentum as your legs swing rightward; tipping your torso toward the left while your feet are tipping toward the right creates momentum opposite to that of the legs — in this way, you don't cause your whole body to fall over even if you tip very aggressively with the feet and legs.

Figure 1-6. *Grip and ski performance are yours when you can change edges, Frames 2–3, without steering or direction change.*

Tipped and balanced

Edge change without direction change

Both dryland and on-snow exercises can be used to build your counterbalancing ability. Here is a preview of one dryland exercise. As with any edge-tipping exercise, dryland or on-snow, start with the boots (or skis) parallel. Keep the boots (or skis) parallel, at the same width apart, and keep both at the same edge angle throughout the tilting. On a carpeted ramp, stand with the boots tipped onto their uphill edges. Then, tilt them through flat, and all the way onto their downhill edges. Maintain balance over your boots by counterbalancing with the upper body. If you can't maintain balance over your feet on a dry, grippy carpet, don't expect to balance comfortably in this exercise on a slippery angled slope. As in all transitions, the difficult moment occurs when the boots are flat on the surface. Less so on the carpet, much more so on snow, this is when it's easy to twist the boots, or tip them unequally.

Many skiers that I observe skiing expert terrain are seriously undertrained in tipping and counterbalancing. One of my fears in writing this book is that such skiers may be tempted to skip the early exercises in each essentials chapter. If you have this temptation, please work through the beginning exercises for each essential, and verify your performance before moving on. If you are already performing these movements, the practice will reinforce these effective movements. If you are not doing the movements correctly or sufficiently, then the early exercises will strengthen them. Critical ingredients for expert skiing include performing all the essentials correctly, and balancing while moving. The exercises in the counterbalancing section will give you the balance you need to be solid in any terrain.

Let's look again at our Sample Turn to see how and where counterbalancing is occurring. Counterbalancing in such turns, when viewed casually, can be elusive — it just looks like my torso stays upright or vertical the whole time. However, this steadiness of the torso belies the movements that it takes to create the illusion of no effort. Such a steady torso is the result of counterbalancing efforts that switch from one side of the torso to the other, just as the tipping switches from side to side.

Figure 1-7. *Start with the fundamentals. These movements and balance are not trivial.*

Figure 1-8. *Counterbalancing highlighted in the Sample Turn (left and right; stretched).*

Frame 1. *The legs are angled to the slope yet the upper body is vertical and the shoulders are nearly level.*

Frame 2. *Upper body is kinked at the hip to lean toward stance ski (outside ski).*

Frame 3. *Shoulders become more level as legs begin bending.*

Frame 4. *Shoulders are totally level with surface; knees are bending under hips.*

Frame 5. *Upper body is neutral in transition, not tipped in either direction.*

Frame 6. *New tipping angles are created upper body begins tilting toward new stance ski.*

Frame 7. *Shoulders are still level although leg and ski tipping has increased.*

Frame 8. *Some upper body inclination is evident but there is still adequate kinking at the hip toward the stance ski.*

Frame 9. *Full angles are achieved, upper body is solidly balanced over the stance ski.*

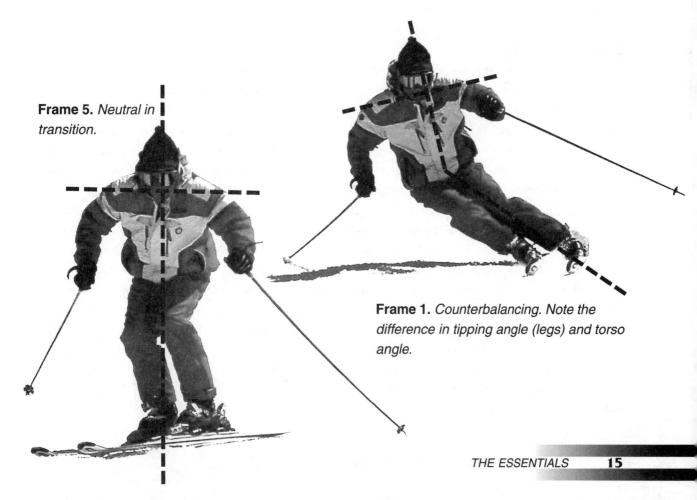

Frame 5. *Neutral in transition.*

Frame 1. *Counterbalancing. Note the difference in tipping angle (legs) and torso angle.*

Figure 1-9. *I've always been told that I ski like an Austrian. My response is, "Thank you. I've heard they're the best in the world."*

Counteracting

Counteracting movements are some of the least understood and the most difficult to teach. Counteracting movements are rotation of the torso around the spine, starting at the hips and lower back, and affecting the whole torso up through the shoulders. Counteracting movements are performed in the opposite direction to what is happening with the lower body. If you tilt your skis onto their right edges, they will arc toward the right, eventually pointing right. A counteracting movement in this case is to turn the torso as though to face toward the left. Your effort is to turn the torso counter to, or opposite to, the direction that the skis will point. The opposite of a counteracting movement is rotation: an effort to turn the torso to face the same direction that the skis will point; in our example, to the right.

When starting a new turn, rotation of the torso (facing the torso in the direction that you expect to go) causes you to reduce your edge angle, reduces the grip of your skis, and often leads to the tails skidding later in the turn. This will compromise your performance in carving and in most situations on the mountain.

Instead, I teach skiers to perform counteracting movements at turn initiation, turning the torso *away* from the upcoming direction of travel. Such counteracting movements augment the grip of the stance ski, allowing the skier to tip and flex into higher edge angles. They also stack the thigh and hip into a strong skeletal alignment, making it easier to resist the turning forces that tend to push you against your stance ski.

Counteracting, counterbalancing, and tipping movements all go together. Working with the three in tandem allows you to develop higher edge angles and the High-C turn entry: balance on your edges above the fall line.

You may see some skiers "skiing into a counter," essentially delaying the counteracting movements until the middle or end of the arc. To do this and still achieve solid balance and edge grip through the bottom of the arc is difficult. I don't recommend trying this approach, especially if you tend to rotate. Gener-

ally, it takes a well-trained athlete who understands and can perform the full spectrum of movements, from rotation, through neutral, to counteracting. Bode Miller knows how to begin turns with rotation — he uses this technique at times on steep slopes — but at the critical part of the turn, when edge hold and pressure on the ski are essential, he quickly performs strong counteracting movements and indeed holds them more strongly than any other skier on the World Cup.

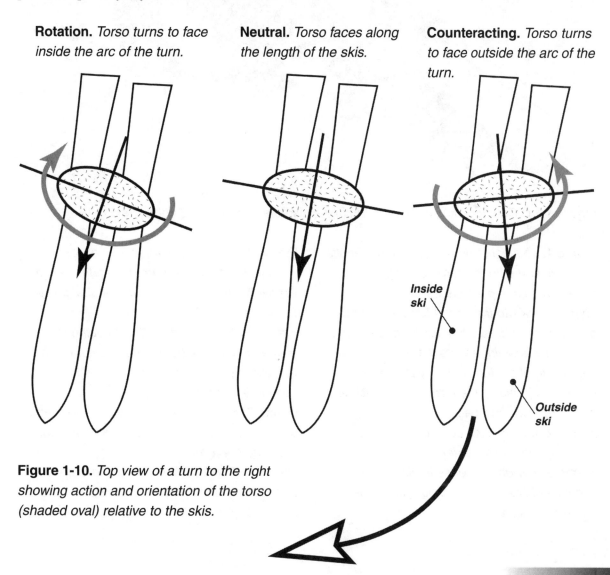

Rotation. *Torso turns to face inside the arc of the turn.*

Neutral. *Torso faces along the length of the skis.*

Counteracting. *Torso turns to face outside the arc of the turn.*

Inside ski

Outside ski

Figure 1-10. *Top view of a turn to the right showing action and orientation of the torso (shaded oval) relative to the skis.*

Figure 1-11. *Counteracting demonstrated in the Sample Turn (left and right; stretched).*

Frame 1. *This figure demonstrates the results of efforts earlier in this turn, starting at transition. In that previous transition, as I tipped my skis to the right, I turned my hips and shoulders to face the left. By maintaining those counteracting efforts, I arrive here, at the middle of the turn, with my inside hip (here, right) leading the turn and the outside hip (here, left), held back.*

Frame 2. *Maintain the counteracting efforts with both hip and shoulder.*

Frame 3. *A slight decrease in hip counter occurs as I flex the legs, bringing me closer to a neutral position.*

Frame 4. *The skis are releasing, almost to flat; my chest is almost square (facing the ski tips).*

Frame 5. *I'm now in a square, neutral position for transition.*

Frame 6. *Just as I have begun tipping to my new edges, I have begun the counteracting movements to face my torso toward the outside of the turn.*

Frame 7. *Stronger counteracting movements ensure that my inside shoulder and hip (here, left) lead the turn.*

Frame 8. *Continued counteracting keeps my torso facing slightly outside the arc.*

Frame 9. *Same to the point of releasing.*

We mere mortals rarely have the skill and strength to change from rotation to counteracting movements in mid-turn, especially at high speed with great forces acting on the body. So, let's leave that advanced technique to the special skiers and instead focus our efforts on coordinating the start of our counteracting movements with turn transition. Learn to use counteracting movements, and once you are comfortable with them, you can vary the timing and amount of them until your ski performance is to your liking.

If you find, in attempting the counteracting exercises, that you cannot counteract, it may be due to a physical reason such as inflexibility in the hips. Flexibility and range of motion in the hips and lower back are necessary if you are to perform counteracting movements in your skiing. Many students become aware of a lack of flexibility in the torso during training of

counteracting movements. When they dedicate themselves to a conditioning program that includes stretching and range-of-motion exercises, and strengthening of the abdominal, lower back, and hip muscles, they make noticeable improvements in their skiing.

Let's take a look at the Sample Turn, and pick out the counteracting movements. You can look at the front of the torso and see what direction it is facing, and how this direction changes. Or, you can imagine a line drawn through both hip sockets. When viewed from above, this line should cross the skis at a non-perpendicular angle (not at 90 degrees). It will only pass through perpendicular at the moment of transition, when the skis are flat to the surface. In a turn to the left, the left hip socket should be ahead of the right, while in a right turn, the right hip socket will be ahead of the left.

The Complete Upper Body

Counterbalancing and counteracting are two different types of movements of the torso. Counterbalancing is tilting the torso from side to side, while counteracting is twisting the torso to face side to side. They use different sets of muscles, and the two activities can be isolated from each other to learn and practice them. In skiing, though, the best performance will be achieved when we can combine both types of movements and perform them together. Chapter 6, The Complete Upper Body, will help you learn to combine and coordinate the movements.

One especially important section of this chapter is on using the poles. How you hold, swing, and plant the poles can help you do what you want with your torso, or it can completely detract from all your best efforts at counterbalancing and counteracting. Pole use depends on movements of the hand, wrist, and arm. One should be able to perform a pole swing and plant that is completely independent, separate, and decoupled from the rest of your movements.

Many skiers never studied or practiced a pole swing — they just ended up with some version of it. In many cases, this pole swing dictates their performance at the end of the turn and through transition. I often ask skiers where their pole is, or where are they swinging it, at a given moment in a turn. Rarely do I get an accurate answer. Usually the answer is a variant of "I don't know. It just happens. I don't think about it."

With advanced skiers, learning to vary and break out of a habitual pole plant has a dramatic effect on their skiing. Once mastered, it is often the breakthrough that leads them to expert skiing.

Proper pole use can make or break an otherwise good series of skiing movements. I find that skiers haven't realized how to develop, focus on, and train independent arm, wrist, and hand movements that will not jeopardize the solid skeletal alignment of the rest of the body.

Figure 1-12. *The High-C engagement is produced by a transition with an edge change, not a direction change.*

In Frames 1 through 3 of this sequence, notice that I am moving the pole and arm, but these movements are not affecting or changing the positions of the shoulder, back, and hip. Too many skiers begin to swing the pole as part of release, and as they swing the pole and arm, they drag along the shoulder, back, and hip. Unfortunately, improper pole discipline can compromise a series of linked arcs.

Even after tremendous effort in my other books to explain pole use, many skiers who come to our camps are not aware of how they use their poles. The reason for this is that pole use is so habitual it requires ongoing performance evaluation, either with a coach or with video, and it requires a concerted effort to make the desired changes. In the chapter on combined counterbalancing and counteracting movements, I'll explain and demonstrate pole use suitable for skiing on shaped skis.

Figure 1-13. *Pole use demonstrated in the Sample Turn (left and right; stretched). With shaped skis, pole use has changed. Now it keeps the skier moving through turns without hesitation.*

Frames 4–7. *After touching the pole on the snow, move that hand forward. This keeps the inside of the body leading throughout the rest of the arc, supporting your counteracting movements.*

Frames 8–9. *The arm swings the pole tip to prepare for the next pole touch. The shoulder and hip are not influenced by the movements of the arm, wrist, and hand.*

Figure 1-14. Harald Harb's Essentials of Skiing *finally delivers the movements you need to master fore/aft balance. Move the feet back in Frames 4–5 to be in balance entering the new turn, Frames 6–7.*

Fore/Aft Balance

Apart from edging and creating angles, which is lateral balancing, the next most perplexing issue for many skiers is achieving and regaining fore/aft balance. I hate to say this, but I rarely think about fore/aft balance when I am skiing. Occasionally I'll notice a lack of fore/aft balance, and then I have to focus. After I pay attention for a few turns, it comes back and once again I'm in balance. If I lose my fore/aft balance, even momentarily, it's because I'm being lazy or I lack overall body tension, which helps keep me in balance. Why is it that I rarely think about fore/aft balance? It's because I practiced the movements that help me maintain that balance so much that those movements are now habitual. Once you learn the best movements to help you maintain fore/aft balance, you can practice them until your fore/aft balance becomes less of a conscious focus.

FORE/AFT BALANCE – IT'S THE LOCATION OF THE HIPS RELATIVE TO THE FEET

In these examples, if you look at the frames before and then after the re-centering, you could easily observe that the hips moved forward. It would then be a short step to think that you need to move your hips forward in transition. Fore/aft balance is a matter of where the mass is (think hips and torso) relative to the base of support (the feet). Therefore, in order to modify

our balance, we need to move the hips *relative to the feet*. That doesn't mean that we're going to move our hips. We are going to learn to adjust the feet relative to the hips.

PULL THE FREE FOOT BACK

In *Anyone Can Be an Expert Skier 1*, I introduced a new idea for re-centering, a movement that I had used in ski racing and coaching for decades, but that was not generally understood in ski instruction: pulling the new free foot back at the release in order to re-center. Even a skier who can already switch edges without the free foot moving forward will benefit from this idea.

When implemented, it will put the skier in a still better position to start the next turn.

Although pulling the foot or feet back may not be an easy, natural movement for you, that doesn't mean you should give up on it. Even if you do not execute it perfectly at first, you should stick with it as an ongoing, conscious activity in your skiing. Why is it that I rarely think about fore/aft balance when I ski? It's because pulling the inside foot back in transition from arc to arc is so much a part of that transition, made so by years of practice, that it has become a subconscious, habitual, and natural movement in my skiing that I want.

Figure 1-15. *Fore/Aft Balance demonstrated in the Sample Turn (left and right; stretched).*

Frame 1. *Balancing mostly on my outside (here, left) foot allows me to move and tuck back the less-weighted inside foot (right) and hold it under my hips as my skis move through the turn.*

Frame 2. *The inside boot is where I want it, but I must maintain a constant rearward tension to keep it under my hips.*

Frame 3. *Since the inside foot is even fore/aft with the stance foot, ski tip pressure is ensured.*

Frame 4. *While the outside leg is bent for the release, the inside boot remains lined up with the stance boot.*

Frame 5. *Both skis are light, therefore pulling the new inside foot (left) back is possible.*

Frame 6. *Inside foot remains light and pull back is strengthened.*

Frame 7. *The tension or pullback is maintained.*

Frame 8. *The tension or pullback is maintained.*

Frame 9. *Boots are lined up fore/aft.*

WHAT ABOUT THE FEET MOVING FORWARD?

Refer to Frames 3 through 5 in the Sample Turn, Figure 1-15. As your skis track through the bottom of an arc, make sure that the weight or pressure you feel on the sole of your stance foot is just behind your arch. If it's on the back of the heel, or if you feel hard contact from the boot cuff on the back of your calf, that's too far back. If you are active in maintaining your fore/aft balance, then you can keep the pressure where you want it, at the back of the arch. If the skis are carving, it is natural for them to move forward through the arc. If you aren't paying at-

tention, this could lead to the skis jetting out in front of you. You should only experiment with fore/aft balance — letting the stance foot move slightly forward, or keeping it held back — on easy slopes, where recovery is safe and speed control is easily maintained.

Now that I've introduced the essentials, and have demonstrated how they appear in the Sample Turn, we're ready to learn and practice each essential. We'll start first with tipping.

Giulia Gianesini, an Italian FIS skier, demonstrates all the essentials: tipping, flexing and extending, counterbalancing, and counteracting. This is the complete game.

CHAPTER 2

Essential — Tipping

THE MOST IMPORTANT ESSENTIAL OF EXPERT SKIING IS TIPPING. Tipping (or tilting) refers to the action and movements of the feet and ankles that pressures the sides of the ski boots and makes them lean to one side or the other. This creates ski and body angles to the snow. The angles necessary for the skis to create a controlled, carved arc are created at the beginning, or transition, and form the High-C part of the arc.

"Practice to become expert at tipping — the rest will be easy."

First practice: Sit in a chair with both feet on the floor, toes pointing straight ahead, feet parallel. Place your hands on your knees and hold your legs firmly to prevent them from swaying back and forth. Tip your feet from edge to edge by prying up on one side of each foot, keeping the other side on the floor. For example, if you are tipping both feet to the right, you should pry the right arch and left little-toe edge off the floor. Tip the feet back and forth, using the hands to prevent the knees from swaying. Tip the feet to the highest angle you can achieve and hold them there for a few seconds. These isolated tilting or rolling movements of the feet are what we call "tipping."

Although tipping sounds very rudimentary, almost boring, it is one of the essentials of expert skiing that most skiers do not possess. Skiers are reluctant to isolate and practice tipping movements, possibly because they don't

Tip as far as you can and balance.

know what to look for or achieve. That is why I will introduce and demonstrate how to practice tipping, to make it your strength. I strongly advise everyone to partake of all the exercises in this chapter. Practicing tipping may not be sexy, but having strong tipping movements in your skiing is very sexy.

"Expert skiers change and create edges by tipping while the skis are under the hips, not by moving the skis out to the side of the body."

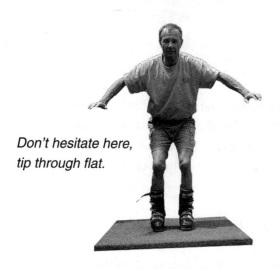

Don't hesitate here, tip through flat.

Most skiers end up on edge by pushing the skis out from under the body, not by tipping the skis on edge and hinging the skis to a higher angle. Tipping the skis to their edges develops edge angles and results in edge grip. When a skier pushes the skis to the side, the skis skid out and eventually reach an angle to the slope. This diminishes the arc because the skis are not gripping. Pushing the skis to the side to achieve edging is hugely deficient in control because the turn is over before the skis start to grip. There is nothing elegant or efficient about this approach, and it doesn't allow you to develop lateral or fore/aft balance.

Keep tipping toward new edges; balance.

Figure 2-1. *Tipping from side to side on carpet in ski boots is a great way to strengthen balance and lower-body movement awareness without snow.*

Start in balance on the uphill edges.

Speed Control

Skiers always ask me how I control my speed. Even on the steepest slopes I seem to be able to control my speed and not fight the slope. I do this by forming the High-C part of the arc. The High-C gives you speed control at the top of the turn so that you can have perfect control at the end of the turn. If, instead, you push your skis to the side to create edge angles, you won't form the High-C part of the turn, and you'll find your skis immediately in the fall line, aiming downhill, upon starting your turn. This means you are accelerating toward the bottom of the mountain, letting gravity increase your rate of descent.

The movements of a High-C entry give you time. You will never feel rushed or out of sorts with the slope again. These movements begin at the feet and then are supported by movements of the mid- and upper-body. These mid- and upper-body movements are the essentials of counterbalancing and counteracting, which will be developed in later chapters. Don't skip to those chapters yet — develop the tipping with your feet first.

Skiers always tell me they lose control in steeps, in bumps, on ice. Only when they take the time to revise their understanding and their movements do they begin to gain control. When they do, it is a beautiful thing to watch.

Like on the slopes, tip through transition.

This is probably the most important balance in skiing.

Figure 2-2. *Practice the High-C edge change at home.*

Shaped Skis Dictate Different Abilities

Modern, shaped skis dictate that expert-level performance is dependent on the ability to get the skis angled onto their edges. Once the skis are tipped on edge, they must be tipped further to increase the edge angle through the turn until it's time to diminish the edge angles back through flat in transition in order to get to the other set of edges. So, tipping includes movements of the feet both to put the skis on edge and increase the edge angle, as well as to diminish the edge angle, bringing the skis back to flat. We call these movements "engaging" to put the skis on edge and increase the edge angle, and "releasing" to decrease the edge angle and bring the skis back to flat. Notice the common theme here: all tipping, no twisting!

If you are really serious about making a difference in your skiing, do not skip any of the exercises to develop tipping. Some skiers might want to thumb through the early sections of the book, eager to get to the "meat." Well, this is the meat — the foundation of high-performance skiing, the serious technique that achieves carving and all-mountain turns. If you perform, practice, and realize the ability to make the movements of the tipping chapter, you will develop into an expert skier.

Johan Brolenius of the Swedish National Team tips to a higher edge angle — engaging. Bending the inside leg assists in reaching a higher edge angle, as you'll discover through the exercises in this chapter.

Indoor Tipping Practice

Indoor practice is your ticket to accelerated performance. Any of the exercises of static tipping on the flats can easily be performed indoors on a carpeted surface. Short, firm carpet is the best for practice, as it feels more like snow. If you can, face a full-length mirror (shower or wardrobe). The feedback of watching yourself is verification of your movements.

In order to practice the exercises of tipping on a sidehill, you'll need to build yourself a carpeted "slope." Take a two-foot-square piece of one-inch-thick plywood, add one or two lengths of 2-by-4 underneath to provide support, and glue or staple carpet on the top surface (a remnant or small kitchen carpet is fine). Prop up one edge about four to six inches and make sure that it is solidly supported, not wobbly. Stand facing the side of the slope that you have created (feet pointing at one of the sides, not toward the "top" or "bottom" of the slope). Again, facing a mirror while practicing is the best for learning. Make sure you perform the exercises facing both directions.

Starting on the flat surface, first practice tipping and holding the boots on edge at the end of your tipping range. Practice this on both sides. Follow the example in the photos by keeping the hands level and out to the side to feel balance.

Tip your feet and combine the hand and arm movements as demonstrated. The idea is to get used to alternating your movement focus from upper to lower body. Practice this so often that you don't have to think about it when you are skiing.

Figure 2-3. *Indoor practice on a carpeted ramp.*

On-Snow Practice

Take these next exercises to the easy slopes first and practice the movements and exercises. Always watch your tracks and if possible bring a friend so you can take video of your tipping sessions. If you dedicate yourself to mastering the exercises demonstrated on these next pages and accomplish the movements with efficiency, you will develop a High-C arc entry with all its benefits, improve your skiing quickly, and notice immediate results.

STATIONARY TIPPING AND BALANCING ON A FLAT SURFACE

In skiing, tipping involves both increasing and decreasing the skis' edge angles. Increasing the edge angle engages the ski edge, then the ski sidecut or design starts to react and create an arc. Decreasing the skis' angle to the snow releases the grip, rolls the skis flat onto their bases, and ends the turn.

In this first, on-snow practice section, we're going to practice tipping movements in a flat area, without sliding. Being stationary means we don't have to worry about speed, control, our direction of travel, or anything other than our tipping efforts.

The first exercises involve tipping the feet and ankles to make the boots lean from side to side, which will tilt the skis from one set of edges to the other. Each time you tilt from one side to the other, your skis will pass through "flat," where the full width of the ski bases sits flat against the snow. In skiing, this happens each time you tilt your skis to switch edges and change direction. **Don't hesitate or pause at "flat"; keep tipping your skis right through flat, onto the other edges.** It's critical to practice this continuous tipping through flat to have the best results in your skiing.

"Tipping is not about turning — it's about balancing."

Figure 2-4. *Continuous tipping through flat, just like the dryland practice, produces dynamic, expert skiing.*

TIPPING WITHOUT TWISTING

If skiers develop an appreciation for how, when, and why things go wrong in skiing, and they learn to manage these situations, success is just around the corner. I will remind you throughout the book that when your skis are flat on the snow, the edges are not engaged, so the skis are vulnerable to twisting (rotational) input from the legs, hips, and shoulders. This stationary exercise of tipping from one set of edges to the other is the basis of turn transitions. In the exercise, we learn the sensations and control needed to tilt the skis without twisting them. Tipping without twisting is required to develop the High-C arc.

Shaped skis are not designed to be twisted, pivoted, or aimed in a new direction while they are flat to the snow. Though many skiers still use this technique, twisting the skis while they are flat to the snow will limit your progress and ability in any situation that requires speed control, control of your direction, or energy efficiency. **Learn to tilt through flat without twisting.**

This book is filled with images of correct movements. None of the transitions demonstrates twisting or pivoting *unless on purpose, to show you what the incorrect movements look like*. Such instances will be well noted.

To see the culmination of the exercises to develop tipping without twisting, look ahead to the Target Tipping exercises (Figures 2-36 & 2-37). In order to achieve the aim of those exercises — tipping from old edges to new while keeping the skis pointed at a target — you'll need to have mastered the earlier tipping exercises in this chapter.

LOOSEN UP THE LOWER BODY

This montage contains three photos from the same series that is featured on the next page. They are overlaid to demonstrate the extreme movement ranges that should be practiced.

In this exercise, the skis remain parallel and "in track" during the tipping. They do not slip from side to side, move toward or away from each other, or twist or pivot. Stay balanced and tip as far as you can to each side, making sure to tip both skis to the same edge angle. Repeat the exercise several times, as the difficulty will soon be increased.

Figure 2-5. *Stationary tipping on a flat surface — use a large range of motion.*

Frame 1. *Begin by tipping both skis to your left as in the photo. Tipping the skis results from foot and ankle movements. Keep the hands, arms, and shoulders level but incline the upper body toward the side* opposite *where you are tipping your feet and skis. Once you have tipped as far as you can, hold this position for a few seconds to practice balancing on the edges. This is the extreme edging position to the left. Notice that the bases of the skis are lifted and not touching the snow. During the exercise, do not stop with the skis flat; stop only with the skis on edge.*

Frame 2. *Gradually flatten the skis.*

Frame 3. *I am just about in neutral, where the ski bases are flat on the snow and the torso is vertical, not tipped, leaned, or angled to the snow. For the exercise, do not pause or stop here. Continue tipping the feet toward the other set of edges (here, toward my right) to create a smooth transition.*

Frame 4. *I have just passed through neutral and am starting to engage the new edges.*

Frame 5. *The goal is twofold — increase the edge angles and maintain balance over those edges by tipping the torso opposite to the feet.*

Frame 6. *Once you reach your limit of tipping, pause for a few seconds to practice your balance. Notice that the torso is leaned or tilted opposite the direction of the feet — this is part of balancing on the edges.*

Figure 2-6. *Stationary tipping on a flat surface. Start on the left edges, and use the feet to tip to the right edges.*

Practice tipping from one side of the skis to the other until you are comfortable with the movements throughout the kinetic chain that are required to perform the exercises. The tipping movements with your feet and ankles are at the base of the chain — they control the rest of your actions. Most skiers find it more difficult to tip toward the outside (little-toe) edge than toward the inside (big-toe) edge, so emphasize this movement to keep the skis tipping to the same angle. The torso should tilt only enough to maintain balance on the edges, no more. The arms and hands can make subtle movements to help adjust your balance.

Explore the influence of the flex or bend of your legs on your tipping results. Tip from side to side with the legs long and extended, then tip with the legs relaxed and more flexed (bent). Compare the range of tipping that you achieve with your legs stiffly extended versus bent and relaxed. Keeping the legs flexible and bent during this exercise increases your range of tipping — this will be important in later exercises.

The skis should not pivot, twist, change direction in any way, or slip sideways during this exercise. The tracks left on the snow by your skis should only be as wide as the bases of your skis. This simple yet challenging exercise is the first step in your quest to improve your skiing through development of the skiing essentials.

STATIONARY TIPPING ACROSS THE FALL LINE

Dryland practice of this exercise is easier because the skis are less likely to slip or pivot on your carpeted slope than on snow.

These exercises build on the tipping and balancing that you practiced in the previous exercise, Stationary Tipping and Balancing on a Flat Surface. In this more advanced version, stand on a gentle hill with your skis pointed across the hill. The flatter the hill, the more similar it is to tipping on the flats. The steeper the hill, the more you'll have to exaggerate and manage your tipping and balancing in order to complete the task.

Standing on a hill in a traverse position (skis pointed across the fall line, not up or down the hill) already places the skis on their uphill edges. As you tip your feet to increase and decrease the skis' edge angles, make sure you stay in place, and do not slide forward or backward. Tipping the skis to a greater or lesser angle while on their uphill edges is similar to the tipping exercise on the flats. Tipping the skis through flat and onto their downhill edges is where this exercise becomes much more challenging. You must tip the torso opposite the feet during this edge change in order to reach the downhill edges and maintain balance on them. This complementary movement of the torso allows you to attain higher angles with the feet, at the base of the kinetic chain. Take a look at some photos in Chapter 4 on Counterbalancing to see this movement at work in advanced skiing.

Figure 2-7. *Dryland practice of stationary tipping across the fall line. Start on the uphill (here, left) edges, and use the feet to tip to the downhill (right) edges.*

HINGING

Hinging is tipping to increase and decrease edge angles while keeping the ski edges in the same groove in the snow. As you stand on the edges, they sink into the snow and create a small groove. Just your body weight on the edges is enough to create this groove. You can slide the skis forward and backward while keeping the skis in the grooves.

Imagine a door that is hanging by its hinges. While you open and close the door, the

Engaging: tipping to higher edge angle →

← Releasing: tipping to lower edge angle

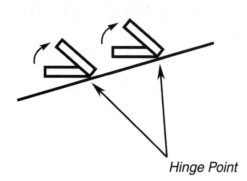

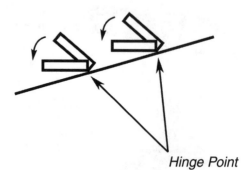

Engaging: *Increase edging*   **Releasing:** *Decrease edging*

Figure 2-8. *Hinging diagram — increasing and decreasing edge angle keeping skis in track.*

edge fastened to the hinges does not slip off the hinges. Similarly, imagine that the edge of your ski that is embedded in the groove is a fixed hinge. You can tilt up and down while the hinge edge stays in place in the groove. If you are on ice, the ski edge doesn't sink as far into the surface as on snow, so you'll have less support from the groove and it will be harder to keep the edge in the groove without slipping out. However, even on the hardest ice, the ski does bite into the surface and create a groove — you just have to move delicately on the icy surface to perform the hinging without slipping.

Practice tipping with the feet to increase and decrease edge angle until you can tilt the skis to a high edge angle and then back almost to flat. The skis should stay in the groove, pointing the same direction without twisting, throughout your hinging. Do not flatten the skis so much that the edges slip out of the groove.

This is not an everyday human movement, so we have to practice it.

LIFTING THE EDGES TO TIP

The way that you think about performing any action influences your success. Take tipping, for example. You can think about tipping in two ways: 1. Lifting one side or edge of the ski away from the snow; 2. Pushing or pressing one edge of the ski down into the snow. If you tend to think along the lines of number two, pushing an edge down into the snow, you might find that it's hard to achieve high angles, the ski tends to skid, and it's hard to balance on that edge. On the other hand, concept one, lifting one edge away from the snow, creates more of an image of balancing on edge above the snow.

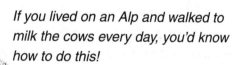

If you lived on an Alp and walked to milk the cows every day, you'd know how to do this!

Figure 2-9. *Dryland hinging practice. Tip up and down through a range of edge angles.*

The next time that you practice tipping, try using concept one — lifting one edge away from the snow. If you are hinging on your uphill edges, as in the previous exercise, think about lifting the downhill ski edge up away from the snow. As you lift the downhill edge away from the surface, the ski base will also lift away from the snow. You'll be left standing on the narrow, metal uphill edge. Think of standing only on the thin sliver of metal that is the ski edge, and don't let any part of your plastic ski base touch the snow. You might find that this approach to edging, this concept, helps make strong tipping to high edge angles more achievable.

Figure 2-10. *Dryland tipping practice on Harb Carvers. You can't push the wheels down into the pavement — tipping is performed by lifting one set of wheels away from the pavement. This is just like tipping skis by lifting one edge away from the snow.*

"You never have to be away from skiing, even if you live far from the snow. Harb Carver practice and dryland boot exercises will keep you sharp."

STATIONARY FULL RELEASE TO NEW EDGES

Once you are comfortable hinging and tipping, the next step is to tip the skis from a high edge angle on the *uphill* edges, through flat, onto the *downhill* edges. This task is challenging and revealing. Maintaining your poise is important as you learn to balance through the transition.

Figure 2-11. *Stationary full release to new edges.*

The importance and relevance in skiing of the movements of this exercise are reinforced each time I watch skiers practicing this exercise at our camps. It is the acid test of readiness for High-C carving and all-mountain skiing. The skiers who can carve, ski bumps in control, and perform High-C turns have little trouble with this exercise. Skiers who cannot perform a stationary edge change across the fall line still have difficulty carving or skiing challenging terrain.

The correlation between success at this exercise and being able to ski at higher levels should tell you something about creating a performance breakthrough for yourself. If you are having difficulty with this exercise, stick with it. Don't give up if you can't perform it right away. Work through the book trying all the exercises; come back and spend extra time on those that you find most challenging. This exercise is valuable enough, and challenging enough, to warrant dryland practice on your carpeted ramp.

Figure 2-12. *Dryland full release to new edges. Stay balanced!*

Frame 1. *Starting position, skis on edge, body well balanced.*

Frame 2. *Use the feet and ankles to flatten the skis. Feel the edge angle with your feet so that you know when they are about to flatten. Watch your skis for verification if you aren't certain of the feedback from your feet.*

Frame 3. *While you tip the skis to their downhill edges, tip the upper body uphill.*

Figure 2-13. *Stationary full release to new edges.*

The stationary full release through transition should only be attempted after you have mastered tipping on the flats, and hinging. There are two challenges in the full release: tipping sufficiently to make the skis tilt all the way onto the new, downhill edges, and maintaining balance over those new edges. Because you are on a hill, and the ground is slanted to one side, you have to tip farther to reach the new (downhill) edges than you do on the flats. Because you have to tip farther with the feet, you have to counterbalance more with the torso — tip the torso opposite the direction of the feet — in order to maintain balance. (Sneak a peek at Chapter 4, Counterbalancing.) The movements to perform this exercise are the same as on a flat surface — the degree to which you have to do those movements is greater on the hill.

The first time you practice stationary full releases, use a very gentle hill — almost flat. Plant your downhill pole in the snow several feet below your skis and hold onto it firmly, as you may need to lean on it to balance before you find out how much to counterbalance with your torso. As always, tip more aggressively with the downhill foot toward its little-toe edge, since this direction of tipping is more difficult. Keep your legs bent and relaxed as you tip. If they are straight or stiff, you won't be able to tip onto the downhill edges. Shift your balance toward the uphill ski (the ski closer to the top of the hill) before you tilt to release.

The critical move for this transition is just before the skis begin to slip. As you reduce the edge angle of your skis, they will keep gripping until they are almost flat on the surface. You have to develop the awareness of the difference in sensation between gripping and slipping, and of how close you are to slipping. Once you start to release the edges, the key is to become aware of when the skis are about to slip; at that moment, you must tip your feet to the new edges without hesitation. If you pause or hesitate at this point, the skis will slip and will probably twist, and you will be unable to tilt to the downhill edges.

Frame 4. *Finishing position. The upper body is counterbalanced and counteracted, in balance over the new edges, and prepared for a new turn. Compare this to the photos in Chapter 6, The Complete Upper Body. If you can start every arc like this, you could win a World Cup some day.*

Figure 2-13 *continued*

Figure 2-14. *This is the montage of Frames 1-3 of the previous sequence, Figure 2-13. It demonstrates the change of edge angles and the change of body position. Note that the skis are parallel, and they remain in the same track throughout the tipping, switching edges without slipping.*

Figure 2-15. *The Stationary Full Release to New Edges is the basis for the High-C turn. Later exercises in the book will build on the release, such as this counterbalancing drill. Your success in those exercises will stem from the groundwork of practice in this chapter. The tipping of the feet is just like on the dryland carpeted ramp.*

Sliding and Tipping

The next stage in difficulty in learning tipping is to add motion — sliding on the snow — and then continue to focus on the same tipping actions that we've practiced up until now. Start on a gentle, open slope. If you can find a location with few other skiers, you'll be able to focus more on practicing the essentials and less on avoiding traffic.

CARVED ARC FROM A TIPPED SKI

The easiest way to experience carving — and we are all about finding the easiest, quickest path to skiing success — is to begin from an edged traverse. Stand in a traverse position, with your skis pointed across the hill, as you did for the Stationary Tipping Across the Fall Line exercise. Aim your skis slightly more downhill than you did in those exercises, since you will want to slide. Tip both skis slightly onto their uphill edges. Hold yourself in place with your poles, so that you do not begin sliding until you are in position and ready. This exercise is like hinging because you start on the edges and you stay tipped on the edges. Don't flatten the skis or they will slip. Focus on the sensation of the skis slicing on their edges.

Observe how the skis are angled to the surface. The lower edges (those closer to the bottom of the mountain) of the skis are slightly lifted from the snow. It doesn't require much edge angle to achieve carving as long as you can balance and avoid any rotational or pivoting actions that produce a torque or twist on the skis.

Notice the upper body. Specifically, my left shoulder and arm seem to be hanging over the left ski and foot. This is not a coincidence. I am tipping my feet and ankles to the right, up the slope. This movement at the bottom of the ki-

Figure 2-16. *Learn to carve by starting the arc on edge.*

netic chain causes my right hip to move or push to the right — a good thing for maintaining the edge angle and balance on the skis. These combined actions keep my skis slicing on edge rather than slipping on the base. Keep both skis in the groove as you did in hinging.

Many skiers lack the ability to carve. This series shows several common technical errors that lead to skidding, rather than carving. Compare the images of this montage to the previous one. Notice that the skis are at different edge angles. The upper ski is not on its little-toe edge, due to a lack of tipping. The skier is turning the lower ski, using the knee and thigh to aim or steer the ski in the direction of the new turn. This causes the edge to lose grip. Remember counteracting movements from the Essentials chapter, Figure 1-10? The hips of this skier are rotated, facing in the direction of the new turn. The torso has also twisted to face inside the arc of the skis, another clue that rotation or steering is being used to turn the skis. These *turning* efforts of the legs and torso result in loss of edge angle and grip. Many skiers use this method, but I call them dead-end movements — ultimately, they will stop your progress as a skier.

Figure 2-17. *Errors in technique will prevent you from learning to carve.*

CARVED ARC FROM A STRAIGHT RUN

Sliding straight downhill on flat skis, then tipping them on edge without pushing them out to the side or twisting them, will be a new experience for many skiers. When you commit to tipping and allow the ski's sidecut to draw you into an arc, there will be new sensations and situations to deal with. Your first impression may be that you are not in control, that the skis are taking you for a ride. This is somewhat true, but with further practice you'll learn to expect and control the ride!

Your initial success depends greatly on your practice of stationary tipping, both on the flats and across the fall line. If you were dedicated to tipping without twisting, especially as your skis passed through flat, then it will be easier for you to engage the skis and balance on them while sliding. Here, you'll be sliding on flat skis before you tip; if you have any hint of twisting, your skis will react. Also, choose a very gentle area for your practice of tipping from a straight run, flat enough that you almost have to push with your poles to keep moving. It needs to be gentle enough that you are not concerned about controlling your speed. Practice one arc at a time, one side or direction at a time. Come to a complete stop and reestablish your starting position before you make the next attempt.

Be aware of how each ski reacts. Initially you may find that the skis want to travel in different directions, either running into each other or away from each other. This has two causes: the skis are at different edge angles, or one ski is more weighted than the other. Try to stand evenly balanced on both feet to maintain similar pressure under each foot. Tip both feet on edge, starting with the foot that tips toward its little-toe edge (this will be the inside foot for the arc).

Success at this exercise isn't a one-time effort. It usually takes a few days of practice with an hour or two per day dedicated to this exercise. Not only are you practicing the movements of tipping and balance, you are also training your feet to recognize the performance of the skis, whether they are slipping on the bases or slicing on the edges. You should identify the slicing sensation from practicing Carved Arcs from a Tipped Ski, page 47. Have fun with your skiing, and keep coming back to practice this exercise until you are confident with your edge engagement. It will have an overall positive effect on your skiing.

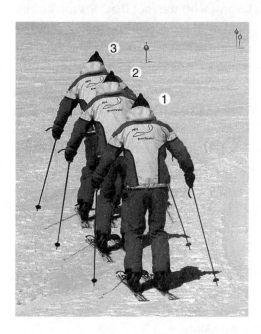

Figure 2-18-A. *Carved arc from a straight run — tipping without twisting from a straight run engages the skis.*

Figure 2-18-B. *Carved arc from a straight run — once the skis are engaged, balance on the edges and ride them through the arc.*

Begin on a gentle slope, facing straight downhill with your skis parallel and flat on the snow. Hold yourself in position with your poles until you are prepared. Lift the poles out of the snow and start sliding downhill with the skis flat.

Begin to tip the inside foot for the arc — here, the right — onto its little-toe edge by lifting the big-toe edge of the ski away from the snow. Keep enough weight on the foot so that the edge leaves a groove in the snow. Just as in the hinging practice, you want to keep the ski edge locked into this groove.

Almost immediately, start tipping the outside ski for the arc — here, the left — onto its big-toe edge by lifting the little-toe edge away from the snow. It, too, needs to leave a groove in the snow. Adjust your arms and upper body so that you stay balanced over your skis. Ride the edges, and wait to see the reaction of the skis.

The skis should carve together on similar arcs, with about the same distance between your feet for the whole duration from start to stop. If they don't, it's one of the two issues I discussed above, different edge angles or different weight. Most often it's insufficient tipping with the inside ski, the one tipped onto its little-toe edge, since this movement is more difficult to perform than tipping onto the big-toe edge. This is the reason for beginning tipping with this inside foot, so it gets a head start on the tipping.

Examine your tracks after performing this exercise. You should see two separate grooves, one for each ski. The distance between the grooves should be consistent from start to finish. The grooves should begin at almost the same place in the arc, and the grooves should aim straight downhill at the very beginning; if the start of the grooves is already aimed across the hill, it means that you twisted when the skis were flat, rather than tipping.

Once you have good control of the beginning of the arcs, making sure that you tip without twisting, then increase the tipping effort through the rest of the arc so that you tighten the radius of your arcs or grooves. This is not an easy exercise, as it requires patience, balance, and finesse in your tipping movements. With diligent practice, you'll develop a new level of balance and skiing performance.

Two Common but Incorrect Versions

PUSHING BOTH TAILS

This is the result of pushing the skis out to the side rather than tipping in order to put them on edge. If you look carefully at the tails of the skis in these photos, you'll see that they are to the left of the ski boots. Correct tipping movements would put the skis on edge directly under the skier's hips, not out to the side.

The arrows indicate where the skis are flat to the snow. Where there is no tipping, there is no arc. Notice how many frames show no arc, no body angles.

Figure 2-19. *Incorrect — both tails are pushed to the side, resulting in a skid.*

THE WEDGE

Many skiers panic when they are in the fall line if they do not feel any resistance to the pull of gravity. In their attempt to regain "control," they push or turn the flat stance ski out from under the body, aiming it across the hill. This causes a skid, which in their mind represents control. There is no tipping, only steering and skidding. These movements do not engage the sidecut of the ski, and will never lead to high-quality skiing. It is for this reason that I suggest practicing on very gentle slopes — you'll hardly pick up any speed, so you'll have less of an urge to rush and panic. Patience with tipping the skis on edge and balancing on them will produce the right results.

Figure 2-20. *Incorrect — the stance ski (here, left) is turned into a wedge position, producing a skid.*

Correct Versions

TIPPING TO BEGIN AN ARC

Figure 2-21. *Correct — tipping the feet without twisting results in clean edge engagement. There is no tail push and no steering of the legs.*

AT SLOW SPEEDS, EMPHASIZE THE FEET

Notice how at slow speeds all the emphasis can be on tipping the skis with the feet. The upper body has little negative influence as long as it is not moved dramatically in the wrong direction.

Figure 2-22. *Correct — the feet tip, the edges grip, and the torso can go along for the ride.*

FULL RELEASE CARVED ARCS

In our sliding practice, our first attempts at carving started on edge and stayed on edge. In the next version, we started flat then tipped to engage the edges. Here is the next more difficult stage: start on edge, release to flat, then tip to engage on the new edges. Of the stationary tipping exercises, this is most like the Full Release to New Edges.

This is a full release while moving. You start on the uphill edges, flatten the skis to release, then tip them to engage the new edges. From that point on, balance and ride on those edges. There are several keys to success. First, start on edge so that you are not slipping downhill. When you start the traverse on edge, the skis will want to arc back up the hill; before they

Figure 2-23-A. *The beginning of a full release carved arc, showing the transition from one set of edges to the other (frames are stretched for clearer viewing).*

Frame 1. *Start aimed across the hill with the skis tipped slightly onto the uphill edges (just enough to keep the skis in a traverse).*
Frame 2. *Slide forward on those edges. Lower the downhill edges toward the snow in order to flatten the skis.*

Frame 3. *The skis are now flat to the snow, but don't hesitate here. Keep tipping toward the downhill edges with the intent of lifting the uphill edges off the snow.*
Frame 4. *The skis are on their new edges, starting to carve the upper part of the arc. Make sure you balance on the edges.*

slow down, flatten and tip to the new edges. Second, do not hesitate or pause when the skis are flat. Simply tip right through the flat phase to avoid twisting or slipping. As in the stationary full releases, keep the legs flexed or bent slightly. If the downhill leg is extended and stiff, you will not be able to tip enough to engage the new set of edges. Focus on balance. Once you have tipped your skis to engage on the new edges, this becomes a game of balance.

Your starting direction on the hill influences the difficulty of the exercise. As usual, choose a very gentle slope. Point your skis almost straight downhill, just slightly toward the side of the hill. This minimizes the amount of time that you have to balance in the High-C arc. If you start with your skis pointed across the hill, perpendicular to the fall line, then you will have to spend a long time balancing in the High-C arc, which makes the exercise more difficult.

Figure 2-23-B. *The same sequence, with the frames in their true positions.*

Advanced Tipping Exercises

In skiing, as your speed increases and the slope gets steeper, you need to increase tipping to reach higher edge angles. It is at these higher angles that the influence of the upper body becomes more relevant. Just as in the stationary tipping exercises, the upper body tips or tilts opposite to the direction of the feet and skis.

EXAGGERATED TIPPING WITH COMPLEMENTARY UPPER BODY MOVEMENTS

Begin tipping with the foot that tilts toward its little-toe edge (here, the right); follow with the foot that tilts toward its big-toe edge (here, the left). At the same time, tilt the torso in the opposite direction, leaning the shoulders to the outside of the arc. Notice in the photos that the inside hand (the right) is lifted aggressively, while the outside hand (the left) is lowered. Remember the concept of lifting the edges and ski bases away from the snow in order to achieve higher edge angles. Pushing the weighted edge down into the snow will only yield a low edge angle.

Figure 2-24. *Tipping the feet to higher edge angles, accompanied by upper-body counterbalancing.*

INCREASE TIPPING THROUGH THE ARC

Figure 2-25. *Tipping the feet to higher edge angles tightens the radius of the arc.*

Notice the tracks in the snow: two clean grooves. When looking at your ski tracks to verify your performance, this is the image you should strive for.

Increasing the tipping throughout the arc will tilt the skis to a higher edge angle, tightening the radius of the arc. In order to increase tipping of the feet to higher edge angles and still maintain balance, you must counterbalance with the torso. If you tip to a higher edge angle without counterbalancing, your balance will shift first to the inside ski, then you'll likely lose your balance to the inside of the turn. This is more obvious at slower speeds and on easier slopes.

Notice that the legs are slightly flexed, or bent, throughout this exercise. If the legs are stiff and straight, you will not be able to tip to higher edge angles. Keep the legs a little bent and relaxed, and you'll be able to tip to higher angles.

Look in Frame 1 at the angle of the torso compared to vertical. It's important to notice and internalize the relationship of the torso angle to the leg angle. If you are standing

Frame 1. *Compare leg and torso angles.*

around in shoes or bare feet, it's normal to hold the torso vertically over the feet — you don't have to think about it. I think this is the reason that many skiers do not move their torso to their advantage in skiing — they're just not used to thinking about it. But once you are sliding on a slope, tipping your skis back and forth and trying to balance on the edges, it's a different story. If the upper body doesn't react in a way to maintain balance, then the benefits of your tipping efforts will be lost. The muscles that pull your ribs toward your pelvis in a lateral crunch or bend are the ones that counterbalance the tipping activities of your feet. Begin using this movement as you exaggerate the tipping of your feet. The carryover into your skiing will be rewarding. You'll develop the counterbalancing essential more in Chapter 4.

HOPPING EDGE CHANGE

Changing edges without twisting or pivoting the skis should be a goal for all PMTS skiers. Learning to isolate your tipping movements from any twisting or steering movements of the legs or torso will let you control exactly what your skis are doing on the snow, whether you want to carve clean grooves or perform a less edged, brushed-carve turn. It's a critical step in the quest to become a complete skier.

If you know how to change your edges for a clean carved turn, and how to ride in balance on these edges, then it's an easy task to learn how to make less edged, brushed turns, or even to pivot. If your technique is based on pivoting and steering, though, it's a long, difficult road to learn how to carve — you won't have learned the isolated tipping movements.

One of the more difficult aspects of learning to tip from edge to edge without a twist is the moment of passing through flat. If we can minimize this time in flat, then it's easier to focus on balancing and keeping the skis slicing along in their grooves and on the changes in

tipping and balancing required at the moment of edge change. It is for this purpose that we use a Hopping Edge Change. We hop at the moment of edge change so that there is no time with the skis flat on the snow. You can't fall into the trap of hesitating at flat, inadvertently inducing a slip or pivot. The edge change is done in the air. By learning a solid takeoff and a solid landing, and minimizing the direction change in the air, it becomes much easier to manage the moment of truth: an edge change without twisting with the skis on the snow.

STATIONARY EDGE HOPS

Since we're starting something new, we're going to take it to its most basic level — here, stationary hopping on the edges. Head for a very gentle slope, like the one you used for practicing Hinging or the Stationary Full Release. We're going to start without sliding so you can just focus on the hop, taking off from and landing on edge.

Hopping requires energy and some leg strength. If you are reading this book in the spring or summer, this might remind you that conditioning is an important part of getting ready for a great ski season.

Stand in a traverse position with your skis pointed across the hill. You don't want to slide forward or backward, so make sure you are perpendicular to the fall line. Since you're standing on a hill, you should be slightly on the uphill edges to begin with. Tip to a slightly higher edge angle by lifting the downhill edges further up from the snow. Keeping your skis on edge, crouch slightly with the legs, then hop up in the air, lifting the skis a few inches from the snow. Hop into the air by extending and pushing with your legs, not by heaving upward with the shoulders and torso. Land on the same edges without letting the skis go flat. Both the takeoff and the landing must be on edge, not flat on the ski bases. Perform several hops in a row on one set of edges. Then, face the other direction on the hill and practice single hops, then several hops in a row, on the other set of edges. We're not changing edges in the air yet, just learning to hold the edges on takeoff and landing. If you takeoff on the left edges, make sure you land on the left edges.

Gauge your performance by looking at your tracks. If you are keeping the skis on edge during takeoff and landing, you'll leave two clean grooves in the snow, just like when you are hinging. If you flatten the skis at any time, they will slip sideways, down the slope, leaving a smudge or even erasing your groove.

Though this sounds simple, the push at takeoff and the impact on landing both require that we increase the strength of our tipping in order to keep the skis on edge. Both the takeoff push and the landing will tend to flatten the skis, diminishing the edge angle. Don't let this happen. Use stronger tipping efforts with your feet and ankles to keep the skis on edge. If you really have a hard time preventing the skis from flattening, you might want to buckle your boots more tightly. If your boots are loose, or too large, it will be hard to hold the skis on edge through the hops.

SLIDING EDGE HOPS

The next added difficulty will be to slide while hopping on one set of edges. On the same gentle slope as for the previous exercises, start in a traverse position with the skis pointed slightly downhill. Tip your skis to a slightly higher edge angle than is provided just by the slope. Hold yourself with your poles until you are positioned and ready, then let yourself slide across the slope on your edges. Crouch, hop, and land as above. Make sure you take off and land on clean edges, leaving grooves in the snow. Make sure to look back at your tracks. It's very easy in this exercise to see whether your skis leave grooves (desired) or only smudges (indicating that the skis flattened).

STATIONARY HOPPING EDGE CHANGE

The next added difficulty will be the edge switch. Head back to your flat, open area where you first practiced stationary tipping. Start by tipping both skis to one set of edges. Crouch, hop with the legs into the air, *tip your skis to the other edges while in the air*, and land on the opposite edges. If you take off from the left edges, land on the right edges. Compare the direction that your skis point at takeoff and landing (look at your tracks — you should see two sets of grooves, right?) Try to take off and land with the skis pointing in essentially the same direction. This is the goal of the exercises — to switch edges without changing direction. The idea of the hop is to eliminate the possibility of hesitating with the skis flat on the snow. The goal isn't to jump as high as you can so that you exhaust yourself.

This is quite a bit harder than hopping and landing on one set of edges. Your first performance goal should be taking off and landing on edge, never flat. This alone demonstrates proficiency at tipping. Once you have mastered this, then turn your attention to the direction that your skis point, working to minimize the direction change during the edge change.

EDGE SWITCH CORRIDOR

Hopping Edge Changes challenge and develop the ability to hold on edge and change edges without the bail-out pivot. Skiers often have a hard time learning to tip continuously through the edge change, especially through flat (when the skis are flat on the snow) — that's the point when things often go wrong.

Hopping Edge Changes reduce your chances of going wrong, as the hop eliminates the flat ski moment. As with every exercise, the benefits you get from it depend on how well you perform the task. Check your tracks of take-off and landing, or have someone video you, to see whether you are cleanly on edge on take-off and landing, and that you minimize the direction change between the two.

Figure 2-26. *Taking off from one set of edges and landing on the other set without going through flat on the snow helps eliminate pivoting and introduces edge-to-edge skiing.*

SLIDING HOPPING EDGE CHANGE

Our next step in difficulty is to slide on edge before we hop. Choose a very gentle slope, just enough that your skis can be slightly on edge for the in-run. You will be switching edges in the air, landing on the opposite edges from the takeoff. Once again, there are several goals: takeoff from edges; land and balance on edges; minimize direction change between takeoff and landing.

Here, skis are placed on each side of the "hop zone" to encourage you to keep the skis pointing in the same direction during the hop.

You could use poles, bamboo, or any other means of creating a corridor. Try to keep your skis parallel to the corridor on takeoff and on landing. If you still tend to change direction in the Stationary Hopping Edge Change, make a wider corridor than shown, or try the exercise without the corridor.

This exercise is not easy, and it does require practice and energy. Mastery represents a high level of tipping and edge control, and of balance. Try it a few times in each direction. If you get tired, take a break, and go back when you are fresh.

Frame 1. *Flex legs while on edge.*

Frame 2. *Hop up with the legs; switch edges in the air.*

Frame 3. *Land on edge, skis parallel to corridor.*

Frame 1. *Pre-takeoff, viewed from the uphill side.*

Figure 2-27. *Sliding traverse to hopping edge change. Main frames viewed from downhill side; insert frames viewed from uphill side.*

Frame 3. *Landing, viewed from the uphill side.*

SKIING ARC TO ARC WITH A HOPPING EDGE CHANGE

Making linked arcs on a slope connected by hopping edge changes is in some ways easier than the sliding and hopping exercises above. If you are strongly on edge during the finish of an arc, the bend of the skis will contribute to your lift-off. You'll find that it takes less effort to hop off the snow if you come at it from a good turn. The requirements of tipping, changing edges, and balancing on edge are still here.

Perform these turns on an easy slope with few other skiers. You'll want a little pitch so that you get rolling, but not so steep that you worry about speed control. At the end of an arc, just before your takeoff for the hop, make sure that your skis are carving on edge, tracking in their grooves, and that your legs are slightly flexed. Extend the stance leg quickly and strongly, then pull your skis and boots off the snow. If you are feeling particularly energetic, try to lift both knees toward your chest. Once you are off the ground, change edges by tipping (lifting up on the previously engaged edges), and get ready to balance on the new edges when you land.

Remember, the performance goal isn't to jump as high as you can — it's to takeoff from edges, land on edge in balance, and minimize direction change during the edge switch.

Figure 2-28. *Overview of arcs linked by a hopping edge change.*

Figure 2-29. *Preparing for the hop: skis tipped on edge, legs slightly flexed.*

Figure 2-30. *Use an energetic extension to hop and minimize direction change of the skis during the edge change.*

Figure 2-31. *Land on the edges needed for the new arc. Note that torso is counterbalanced and counteracted in order to balance on the landing edges.*

Figure 2-32. *Finish the turn by riding around the arc on the edges and bending the legs slightly to prepare for the next hop.*

It's important to remember that the hopping here, as in all the Hopping Edge Change exercises, is an effort of the lower body. Avoid bending at the waist and lifting with the shoulders. During the hop, the upper body must tip laterally, opposite the direction of the feet, in order to maintain balance in the air and upon landing on the new edges. If you keep your torso strong and steady when you land, it will help the skis engage. If the torso is limp and falls forward, it will make it hard to land in balance on the edges. Don't panic when you land — the skis will grip and arc, making it easier to balance.

TAKING THIS EXERCISE BACK INTO SKIING

Now that you are huffing and puffing from all of the hopping, how should you proceed to take the benefits you have derived from this exercise back into regular, no-hop skiing? Stick with the hopping, but reduce the height of each hop and the time you spend in the air. Keep the same attention to the strong edging and balance at takeoff and landing, switch quickly in between while keeping the skis headed straight (no direction change), but don't try to hop off the ground. First it'll be a regular hop, then a mini-hop, then a micro-hop, then an imaginary hop. If you keep the rest of your efforts consistent, you should bring the clean edge change and balance on your edges from the hopping exercises into your free skiing.

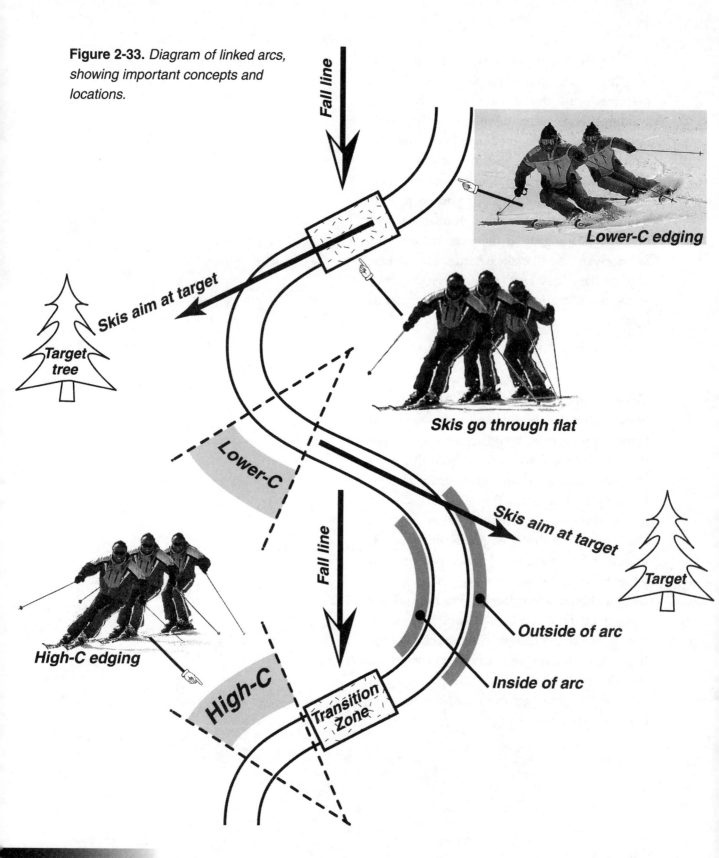

Figure 2-33. *Diagram of linked arcs, showing important concepts and locations.*

Fall line

Lower-C edging

Skis aim at target

Target tree

Skis go through flat

Lower-C

Fall line

Skis aim at target

Target

High-C edging

High-C

Transition Zone

Outside of arc

Inside of arc

HIGH-C ANGLES

Figure 2-34. *High-C angles put you "upside down" to the hill.*

The High-C portion of an arc is above the fall line, when the skis are still heading outbound on the new edges. This is often referred to as being "upside down" on the slope, since you are standing on the downhill edges and the body is downhill of the skis. If you were just standing on a hill, you would certainly choose to stand on the traditional edges, with your body over your skis. You wouldn't try to stand in the High-C position!

To change edges into the High-C means that you'll be tipping the skis from their uphill to their downhill edges. You'll need to counterbalance with the torso, effectively leaning the shoulders uphill.

Figure 2-35. *The upper body doesn't influence the skis (no direction change of the skis) through two-footed transitions. Weight is more equal between the skis until engagement is achieved.*

TWO-FOOTED RELEASE

Achieving a High-C turn requires a patient transition, performed solely with lateral tipping of the feet, with no rotational, pivoting, or steering movements that compromise the engagement of the skis. Compromising movements originate primarily in the upper leg (thigh), torso, and shoulders. All of the tipping exercises presented so far in this chapter work toward accomplishing the High-C edge change. If you have worked at them and verified your performance, your feet are ready to perform High-C tipping.

TARGET TIPPING

One of the goals of this chapter is to learn to tip the skis without twisting them, especially during edge change. Keeping the skis pointed at a target on the side of the slope while changing edges is a cue to help you to minimize direction change of the skis, and to help you verify your performance. The goal is to eliminate as much steering or twisting of the skis as possible, so that you engage the skis in a High-C arc. A solid turn transition is dependent on your tipping movements, which you can build through the exercises in this chapter. When you have the confidence to release and engage on any slope, your skiing will skyrocket.

In target tipping, whatever object your skis point toward at the end of your arc, just before you change edges, becomes the target. You'll have a new target for each arc you make, on alternate sides of the slope. Large objects are better than small ones since they are easier to see. Once you know your target, change edges and keep the skis pointing at and sliding toward the target. There should be a brief moment at the start of the new arc when the skis are engaged on their new edges, still pointing at the target.

TARGET: LIFT TOWER

Figure 2-36. *The lower body changes edges and prevents direction change of the skis until the new edges are engaged. The release of momentum from one turn and engagement of the sidecut in the snow influence the initiation of the new arc.*

Figure 2-37-A. *The stance leg is extended but the release begins with flexing the stance leg and tipping the stance foot. Notice how the hips are lined up over the ski boot, maintaining fore/aft balance on the steep slope.*

Figure 2-37-B. *The target is straight ahead. The skis release and continue to point at the target, as the tails follow the track created by the tips. The tails do not move uphill (which would indicate a heel push or pivot.)*

Figure 2-37-C. *From release to engagement without redirecting the skis.*

Conclusion and Comments

Tipping is the single most fundamental movement in skiing. The rest of the essentials contribute to overall skiing performance, and we will build them through the rest of the book, but you'll find as we go along that most of the other essentials complement the tipping actions of the feet. When you add counterbalancing, you'll do it in proportion to your tipping, and in order to maintain balance while tipping. The faster you tip your feet, the quicker you'll need to perform your counteracting movements. Without competence in the essential of tipping — tilting the feet without twisting, using the feet to sense the engagement or release of the skis — the rest of the essentials cannot produce good skiing. Tipping is the basis for good skiing. The rest of the essentials, when coordinated with tipping, simply make it better.

Hans Grugger of the Austrian National Ski Team demonstrates High-C angles. The arrow shows the top of the arc leading into the fall line.

CHAPTER 3

Essential —
Flexing and Extending

A S YOU CAN SEE IN THE PHOTOS AND MONTAGES IN THIS BOOK, skiing involves a lot of flexion (bending) and extension (straightening) of the legs, especially in transition between connected arcs. In PMTS technique, each leg has a different role. At the bottom of the arc, just before release, the previous stance leg starts to flex aggressively both to initiate the release and then, as it becomes the inside leg for the new arc, to develop the tipping angles for the new turn. At the beginning of the new arc, the previous inside leg becomes the stance leg. It will extend in the new arc, but only once the skis are engaged on the new edges and the body starts to move inside as a result of the free foot flexing and tipping.

> *"Actively flex the inside leg for the coming arc; let the extension of the new stance leg be passive."*

Flexing the inside leg (along with tipping) moves the torso into the center of the arc. As the inside leg flexes to move the body into the center of the arc, the outside leg extends to keep the stance ski in contact with the snow. The extension of the outside leg is not the motivator for moving the body; there is no effort to push the body inward through the extension of the stance leg, though it may look like that in photos or when experts ski.

In this chapter we'll be talking about flexing and extending. However, tipping is used in conjunction with them, so adequate performance of the exercises in the tipping chapter is a prerequisite for some of the exercises here.

Timing of Flexion: Traditional Instruction Starts You Out Wrong

Flexing and extending are important throughout linked turns, but they are critical in the most important part of linked arcs: the transition. The timing and movements for transition taught in traditional ski instruction are opposite to those used by experts. If you learn them from the beginning, you'll have incorrect timing and it will cause problems later in your skiing when you want to become an expert. Getting out of these dead-end movements takes effort and time. Even traditional ski instructors often do not realize that they push off, and have "up" movements and extensions in transition built into their skiing. Maybe that's the standard, so it's acceptable, but it's not the road to expert skiing.

In traditional instruction, you are supposed to rise at release, which is an extension of the legs. Once the legs extend, they must quickly sink into flexion in order to dig the edges in by the end of the turn. This is needed to reduce the speed that was picked up by standing up, away from the edges, at transition.

Whenever there is an upward extension, pressure is transferred to the skis. This makes it harder to tip the skis on edge. You have to wait until you begin sinking or flexing down to begin real tipping, which delays edge engagement. The flexing that follows leg extension can only occur during the turn, which is too late. As well, flexing reduces pressure on the skis, not what you want to help tighten an arc.

Needless to say, this interrupts momentum from one arc to the next, making it hard to create smooth transitions. This is frustrating for skiers and instructors alike if they are looking for smooth transitions.

PMTS in Comparison

The beauty of PMTS technique is that with flexing and tipping used to produce the turn transition, you gain a solid arc; this arc creates the momentum to make it easy to begin the next arc. With the timing of PMTS technique, flexing the downhill leg to release lets momentum create the transition, so you don't have to add effort to start each turn. The big difference between PMTS and traditional technique is that in PMTS, you already have an edge angle when you begin flexing or extending, while in traditional technique, flexing and extending are done with little or no edge angle. In traditional technique, the skis are often slightly on the *old* edges when extension begins.

TRANSFORMATION

Many skiers tell me when they learn to transition and link turns with PMTS technique that they feel like they aren't doing anything. That's what I like to hear: quality skiing is about simplicity, efficiency, and conservation of energy. If you have learned traditional flexion and extension movements, it will take a rearrangement of your thinking and your movement sequence to achieve this new efficiency.

Flexing and Extending

Flexing and extending are both addressed in this chapter. However, in my years of observing skiers, I have found that the majority need to spend more time working on flexing. Flexing is the essential that most skiers need to enhance or increase; extending develops easily when flexion is timed and performed correctly.

Flexing means bending the leg. In skiing we want to bend the leg at all its joints: the ankle, knee, and hip. Extending means making the leg longer, or straightening it at all the joints. Flexion and extension work in tandem: without one, you can't have the other. Without extension, you cannot bend the leg very far. Without flexion, you cannot extend the leg any further. Few skiers use a large enough range of flexion and extension of their legs in skiing, so the exercises of this chapter will develop your ability and comfort to work with a greater range of motion. The timing of these movements and where they happen relative to the turn arc are critical to your skiing success, as is the coordination of flexing and extending with your tipping movements. There are plenty of exercises in this chapter which will help you coordinate your flexing with your tipping for best effect.

Flexing and extending are actions of the legs, but they require some cooperation with the upper body. To achieve deep flexion requires some forward bending of the torso to stay in balance (see Figure 3-1, Frame 1). The torso will need to tip from side to side — counterbalancing — through each arc to keep you balanced laterally. The more you flex and tip with the inside leg to reach deep edge angles, the harder you need to counterbalance with the torso. The side-to-side tipping requires tension in the muscles on the stance side of the torso, like a lateral crunch, and you will often feel stretching of the muscles on the inside (free foot side) of the torso. We'll focus on the torso in the Chapter 4, Counterbalancing. Let's get on with the legs!

Figure 3-1. *Frame 1, exaggerated flexing. Frame 2, exaggerated inside leg flexion and outside leg extension.*

Exaggerate while Learning

Since most skiers use very little flexion while skiing, practicing any amount of flexing feels like a lot. At our camps, many skiers learning to flex would swear that they are flexing a huge amount. When they watch video of their efforts, they realize that while it felt like a lot, it only looks like a little. These same skiers are astounded at what they can achieve and how their skiing improves when they exaggerate their flexing practice.

Similarly, be prepared to exaggerate while practicing the exercises in this chapter. Exaggeration will help you to use your full range of motion, and will help you to become accustomed to a very different range of motion. It's very helpful to watch video of yourself and compare it to the images of the exercises, to make sure you are flexing as much as you'd like.

Boot Touch Exercises — Ski Yourself into Flexing Ability

The next series of exercises helps you learn to flex, to coordinate flexing with tipping, and to start a turn with your legs flexed. If you have the traditional up-down pattern, these exercises will start to reverse that movement pattern for you. They may look extreme, but they work to break old habits.

In this exercise sequence you'll see that I am touching the tops of my boots. The goal in flexing is to bend the legs — ankles, knees, and hips — so make sure you bend your legs as much as you can to accomplish the deep flexion shown here. It's not valuable to keep the legs stiff and simply fold forward at the waist.

If you aren't able to bend your legs enough to touch your boots, then reach for the sides of your knees instead. The objective is to learn to bend the legs. Touching the boots is only the confirmation.

If you aren't confident with the flexing, start by practicing the flexing without sliding. Go back to the flat area in which you practiced stationary tipping, and reach down to touch your boots (or the sides of your knees, if you've chosen that landmark). Extend the legs to stand up, then reach down again. Repeat this several times until you know how much to flex.

Figure 3-2. *In a traverse, flex to crouch then stand up again; stay on the same edges throughout.*

FLEXING AND EXTENDING WHILE STAYING ON EDGE

Find an open, gentle slope with little traffic. Start in a traverse with your skis aimed slightly downhill. Hinge your skis on their edges before starting — you want to start and keep the skis in grooves for the whole exercise. Once you are slicing along on both edges, crouch down and touch the boots as in the photo. Touch and stand several times going across the hill. Make sure your skis always stay on edge, whether you are flexing or extending. Perform this in both directions across the hill.

Figure 3-3. *Begin in a traverse, Frames 1–3, by bending and touching your boots. Tip your skis while touching your boots, Frames 4–5.*

TOUCH AND TIP

Stay on the same slope as the previous exercise. Make these arcs one at a time, from the starting traverse, through the arc, until you stop. Reestablish the starting edges for the next version while stopped.

Start traversing on edge, as in the previous exercise. Crouch down and touch, stand up, then crouch and touch again. On the second touch, keep your hands on the boots and tip the skis through flat onto the new edges. Stay crouched and touching the boots until your skis are headed straight downhill; then you can extend and stand up until you arc to a stop.

This is just like a Full Release to New Edges in Chapter 2, Tipping. Go from one set of edges to the other without any twisting, and leave two grooves in the snow on the new edges. The difference here is that your legs are deeply flexed for the whole transition.

The timing of the tipping relative to the flexion is important. Many skiers try to tip or turn the skis while their legs are still extended, before they flex to touch the boots for the second time. If you can talk out loud or in your head, the words to accompany your movements should be "touch - stand - touch - then - tilt." Having the "then" gives you a little pause while you touch for the second time, ensuring that you are flexed while balanced on the uphill edges. Then, tilt to the new edges. The goal here is to develop the ability to tip and balance with your legs flexed.

Figure 3-4. *Extending begins in Frame 3 of the sequence.*

EXTEND WITHOUT JEOPARDIZING THE BALANCE ON THE NEW EDGES

This is the continuation of the previous exercise. When you are first performing those turns, focus on the flexing and tipping at the transition. Don't worry too much about the rest of the turn. Once you have good success with the transition, going edge to edge in balance, then it's time to think about how you extend after the flexed transition.

Start exactly as before. When your skis have arced until they are pointing straight downhill, slowly stand up by extending your legs. Be patient as you stand up. Make sure that both skis stay in their grooves as you stand up, and that you do not lose your balance toward one side or the other.

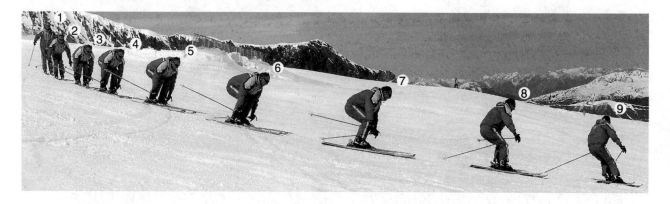

Figure 3-5. *Stand or extend before the next traverse begins as in Frame 9.*

LINKED TURNS WITH DEEP FLEXION

Practice individual turns, coming to a complete stop after each arc. When you can consistently start on the edges, double touch, tilt to the new edges, then ride the edges and stand up, you'll be ready to link turns. Once you extend and are riding the edges, that will be just like the beginning traverse for the next iteration.

Take your time and remember to talk yourself through the new movements, as this is help-ful in establishing the new rhythm and timing. Linking turns is the time when you are most likely to pull out your old rhythm and movement pattern. The goal is to join arcs as is demonstrated on the DVD that accompanies this book. Coordinating the flexing and tipping with the arcs is the challenge here. Having a friend video you is helpful in seeing your progress.

Tuck Turns without Standing Up

Figure 3-6. *Linking turns in a tuck encourages you to keep the legs more flexed than usual, especially through transition.*

Linking arcs while in a tuck position can be practiced by all levels of skiers. Tuck turns can be performed with many different focuses. Here, the focus is to keep the legs flexed, and to prevent standing up in transition. When the upper body is locked into the tuck position, it can no longer be used as a surrogate for flexing and tipping. If you normally use even a subtle up and rotation with the torso to start turns, this exercise will help to eliminate it so that you can focus on the lower body.

Figure 3-7. *Tuck position: lower the upper body, keep the arms extended, and squeeze the elbows in.*

STATIONARY TIPPING IN A TUCK

Practice the tuck position and tipping in the tuck before you start sliding. On a flat area, or very gentle hill, get into a tuck. Flex the legs, bend the torso over so that the chest is low, hold the arms out in front of you with the hands held together and the elbows squeezing the poles against your sides. This tension with the arms holds the body as a unit, important for this exercise.

Holding your tuck, tip your feet back and forth. All the performance requirements from Chapter 2, Tipping, still pertain to your tipping once you are in a tuck.

TUCK TURNS

Most skiers can perform tuck turns on easy terrain. Head back to Chapter 2, Tipping, to the Carved Arc from a Tipped Ski, Carved Arc from a Straight Run, and Full Release Carved Arcs. Try these exercises again, holding your tuck position. When you can perform them well, with the feet tipping and engaging the skis, then link several arcs together. Maintain the tuck position throughout.

Figure 3-8. *Keep the hands touching during tuck skiing. When viewed from above, your poles make a "V" from the pole grips together to the baskets behind you. Point the hands — the base of the V — at the stance boot.*

TIPPING IN TUCK WITH COUNTERACTING

This more advanced version of tipping the feet while in a tuck involves a counteracting movement of the upper body. Point the "V" of your poles opposite to the direction of tipping. If your feet are tipping to the right, aim your V to the left. The will keep the V aimed out toward the stance foot (toward the foot tipped onto its big-toe edge). Start with stationary practice, then add it to your linked tuck turns.

Frame 1. *My skis are tipped to the left, so I point my hands to the right, toward the stance foot.*

Frame 2. *I tip the skis to the right, to release them.*

Frame 3. *I am tipping through flat. At this neutral point of edge angles, the poles should also reach neutral: aiming straight forward.*

Frames 4–5. *Keep tipping the feet toward the right, while aiming the poles to the left.*

Figure 3-9. *Tuck turns with counteracting — point "V" of pole toward stance boot.*

Tipping and the Roles of the Inside and Outside Leg

In the upper, High-C portion of a turn, the inside leg flexes (bends) to increase edge and body angles, at the same time as the inside foot is tipping toward its little-toe edge. The outside leg is extending to maintain ski-snow contact.

In the lower part of the arc (the "Lower-C"), the inside leg stays flexed in preparation for transition. Because the outside leg has been lengthening through the arc, it can bend to start the release, giving in to (but not collapsing under) the forces of the turn. Once the turn is sufficiently completed, the stance foot will start to tip toward its little-toe edge, diminishing the edge angle of that ski, moving the body over the skis for the transition.

You can easily see how the flexing and tipping actions have to work together. So, this chapter will be most helpful for your skiing if you already have a reasonable ability to tip the skis to release and engage, developed in the previous chapter. The timing of flexing and extending depends on the tipping and engagement of the skis. It doesn't make much sense to extend or flex if your skis are flat — that will just move your body up and down, and won't create any arc.

In the single frame to the right (Frame 5 of the Sample Turn), the skis are very close to flat and both legs are flexed (bent). This is a good starting point to explain flexing and extending for this chapter. As always in PMTS technique, the active side of your body is the one that you will move *toward* in the resulting turn. If you are about to turn left (as in the photo), then your left leg and foot should be your focus. Increased flexing of the left leg and tipping of the left foot toward its little-toe edge begin the arc. The tipping and flexing of the left foot and leg pull the torso toward the left, to the inside of the new arc. The right leg has to stretch out, or lengthen, in order to maintain contact with the snow. If you look at Frames 6 and 7 you will see the outside (right) leg straightening, extending. Think of this action as reaching the foot to the snow, not as pushing away from the snow.

Figure 3-10. *Transition, the one point where both legs are flexed the same amount.*

Figure 3-11. *To many observers, it might appear in Frames 5–7 that I extended my outside leg in order to push my body to the inside of the arc. Nothing could be further from the truth! Flexing the stance leg at the end of the previous turn (the release, Frames 2–3) enabled my momentum to send my body into the new arc. Extending the stance leg is merely to maintain contact. Continued flexing with the now-inside leg pulls my body further inside the arc.*

After transition, headed into the High-C arc, the inside leg continues to flex. It needs to fold up under the hips to get out of the way and allow the hips to drop closer to the snow. The inside thigh is often parallel to the snow in aggressive turns, indicating a lot of flexing of the inside leg. A straight leg measures 180 degrees (the angle between the thigh and the shin). By Frame 5 of this arc, the inside leg is flexed to about 125 degrees — close to a normal squat position. By Frame 7, the inside leg is flexed almost to 90 degrees, and the outside leg is almost totally extended. Remember, the outside leg extends just to keep the ski in contact with the snow. Once the skis are in or beyond the fall line, into the Lower-C portion of the arc, the outside leg will become weighted or loaded.

Figure 3-12. *The extended outside leg resists the load from arcing through the Lower-C.*

Coming into the load portion of the arc, at the fall line and lower, the outside leg is going to have to support the loads generated by arcing. It is better to take this load or pressure with an extended stance leg. When the leg is extended, Figure 3-12, most of the load can go up through the leg bones — this is known as being skeletally aligned to the force. If the leg is bent or flexed when it has to support the turning load, then the muscles will get a workout trying to prevent the leg from being flexed further.

The beginning of the release reverses the roles of the legs. The previously extended stance leg flexes or bends to move our bodies closer to our feet, then over our skis and into the new arc. Our momentum in the turn wants to bring our body downhill. Keeping the stance leg extended resists this momentum and keeps us in the arc of the turn. When you flex the downhill leg and add some tipping to flatten the stance ski, it is this momentum that brings the body over the feet to the neutral position of Figure 3-10, Frame 5, and then further into the new arc. In quality skiing you can completely control the rate and direction of motion of the center of mass (torso) through flexing and tipping.

My Emphasis on Ski Angles Continues...

When your skis are on edge, you have angles. Once you have angles, you can flex one leg and extend the other. If you are on edge, your skis are slicing and you can balance and ride on those edges. I demonstrated this in the previous chapter on Tipping. I emphasize it again because it represents solid skiing. Creating angles by moving the body inside the skis' arc does not mean that you are about to fall over. Skiing with angles brings a sense of edge hold, stability, and connection to the snow. Expert skiers ski on edge because it is stable and provides control of speed and of the skis.

Figure 3-13. *From an extended stance leg in Frame 1, through transition, to new extended stance leg in Frame 6. Frame 6 is the classic High-C arc — high edge angles above the fall line. This is referred to as being "upside down" on the slope.*

Changing Your Timing

Part of the reason that skiers don't flex is that they are habituated to the wrong timing of flexing and extending. Flexing more, but at the wrong time, doesn't produce much benefit. This is a deadlock in skiing progress. It will take a reversal of movement and timing to have a true arcing experience.

In any sport, changing anything to do with timing can be very difficult. The exercises presented here have proven in our camps to be very effective at reversing traditional up-down movements. Within a few sessions of diligent practice you should be able to maintain the new timing in your free skiing. Once the reversal of the traditional up-down pattern has taken hold, the world of skiing shines brightly. Once you can coordinate flexing with your release, you'll be able to absorb bumps, finish turns in time, release your edges, and control your speed.

Monika Bergmann-Schmuderer of the German National Ski Team demonstrates the actions of the legs from the Lower-C arc through release. In Frame 1, she's holding on edge with the inside leg flexed, the outside leg extended. In Frame 2, she flexes both legs slightly to assist in tightening the turn arc. In Frame 3, transition, she has flexed the old stance leg until it is even with the inside leg.

When Should Legs Flex/Bend?

When you are first learning to flex and extend, you'll be thinking about when to perform the movements relative to where you are in your turns. It's thus important to have a certain spatial awareness while skiing. Take a look at Figure 3-14. There are two quantities that you should know at every moment: 1. Your direction of travel; 2. The direction that your skis point. With this information, you'll know when your skis are approaching the transition zone — time to release!

If you are carving — truly slicing on the edges at all times — then you will always travel in the direction that your skis are pointing. If you still sometimes skid or pivot, then there are moments when your skis are pointing in one direction while they and you are traveling in another.

Knowing where you are on the hill and relative to your turn arc is the first way of judging your timing of release. Once you have some competence at flexing and at tipping, you'll have another way to judge when to release: you'll time your release according to the pressure building under your skis. When I feel the load building under my skis, when they start to push back at me, I know that they are engaged in an arc. Just before my skis slice across the hill (there's a spatial reference), I initiate release with a controlled flexing of the downhill leg. I gauge how much and how quickly to flex by feeling the pressure under the ski — it's part of my feedback.

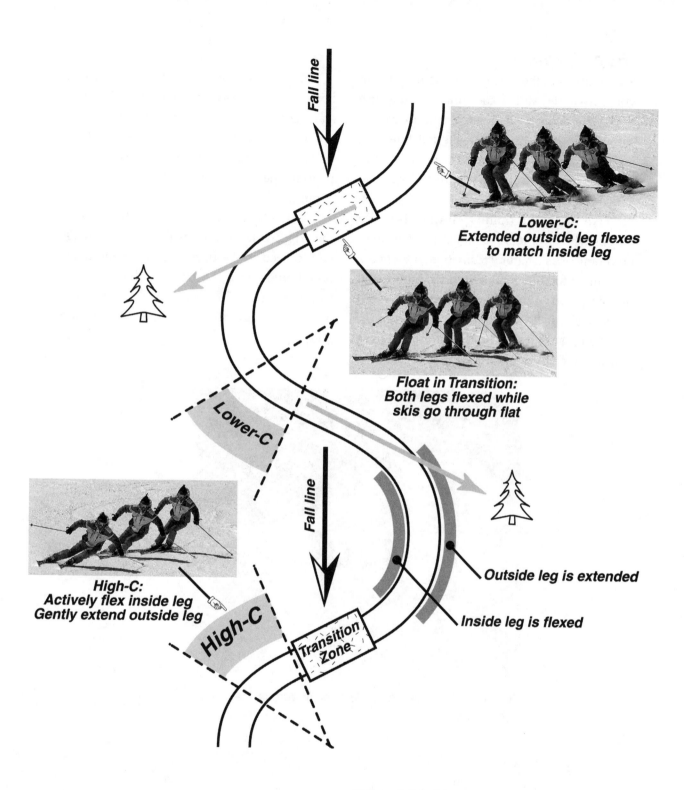

Fall line

Lower-C:
*Extended outside leg flexes
to match inside leg*

Float in Transition:
*Both legs flexed while
skis go through flat*

Lower-C

Fall line

High-C

High-C:
*Actively flex inside leg
Gently extend outside leg*

Transition
Zone

Outside leg is extended

Inside leg is flexed

Figure 3-14. *Diagram of turn arcs showing
locations of flexing actions relative to arcs.*

Ridge Turns

Ridge turns are the next exercise that will help you learn to flex, and to coordinate flexing with tipping to achieve the release. The ridge is a snow berm that runs down the fall line, and it's large enough that you need to bend your legs as you ski across it to avoid getting launched into the air.

We use ridge training at our Harb Ski Camps whenever it is available, either through grooming or as a natural formation. If there is a ski trail on top of a mountain ridge with a trail that drops off to the side, this transition often works well for flexion training. At our camps, we often plant little brush tips on the ridge as indicators for turn and flex timing.

If you are a novice, just skiing across the berm without losing your balance is a good starting point. Then, start to flex your legs as you cross it. Your head and shoulders should travel at the same height as you cross the ridge. If your head pops up, your legs didn't flex enough.

When you are confident to try turns on the ridge, make your transition right on top. As you learned in the tipping chapter, the transition should be made by tipping the feet, not by twisting them. The ridge encourages you to bend your legs at the same time as you are tipping.

Figure 3-15. *Traverse or ski directly across the hump the ridge provides.*

Figure 3-16. *Suck up or retract both legs before the ridge can pop you into the air.*

Figure 3-17. *Finish the previous turn before skiing into the ridge.*

Figure 3-18. *Change edges without a direction change as close to the top of the ridge as possible. Extend the outside leg on the other side of the ridge.*

Add Flexing and Extending to Tipping for Higher Edge Angles

When I think of quality skiing, the image is of arcs that connect smoothly with each other, not of interruptions in transition. Properly timed flexing, coordinated with tipping, is a key to the smooth and easy transition between turns.

In most cases, if you extend one or both legs, you will apply pressure through the bottom of your foot to the snow or ground. If you extend with your ski flat on the snow, your body will move up. This is not desirable for edge tipping or transition. If you extend with your ski on edge, your torso will move to the side at an angle away from your foot. On a slope, while sliding downhill, if you extend with one leg and flex with the other, your body will move toward the flexing leg. You can add tipping of the free foot into this mix with good effect. Flex one leg and tip to the little-toe edge, and your body will move further in that direction. You can also combine just the flexing and tipping, and not add the effort of extending, and your body will still move to the side.

Experiment to find the best results once you're on edge. Try not to extend during transition; keep both legs flexed the same amount. If you tip and extend, but you don't flex the inside leg, then you'll only be able to develop small edge angles. What happens to your balance if you overextend the outside leg, compared to gradually flexing the inside leg? Both movements will move your body to the side, but the overextension is harder to control and is more likely to make you lose your balance to the inside.

To experiment with flexing, tipping, ex- tending, and their influences on you, choose an easy hill where you do not need to make turns in order to control your speed. Start each attempt by sliding straight downhill on flat skis. In this situation, as compared to linked turns, there are no turning forces to help you to move from side to side. You can truly investigate the influence of the different movements.

In order to create an arc from a straight run, focus on the side in the direction you'd like to go. If you want to arc to the left, flex the left leg and tip the left foot to its little-toe edge. Keep that inside ski on the snow as you flex, with just enough weight to engage it and make a slight groove in the snow. Don't push hard or lean on it or you'll lose your balance.

The Weighted Release, introduced in *Anyone Can Be an Expert Skier 2*, is a form of pressuring the inside ski at the initiation of turns. Developing and controlling balance on one ski are significant parts of the exercises in that book. If you have practiced some one-footed balance on both big-toe and little-toe edges and transferring balance, you're ready to practice shifting balance from foot to foot through turns. When you are first working on this versatility of pressuring, it can be helpful to use a short, very shaped, flexible ski, as it will engage quickly and create tight arcs with only a little input from you. A junior slalom race ski is a good option, in a 145-155 cm length. Go through the tipping exercises, then the flexing exercises, then combine tipping and flexing. For many skiers, carving is achieved in a day or two using these skis and this exercise approach.

Figure 3-19. *Flexing does not have to be extreme to get tipping and carving.*

FLEXING AND EXTENDING IN FULL RELEASE CARVED ARCS

Here is an exercise that you first performed in the Tipping chapter. You can use this exercise as a basis for experimenting with flexing the inside leg and extending the outside leg. Link together several Full Release Carved Arcs. Make two clean grooves in the snow, and try to keep the grooves parallel and an equal distance apart. Remember that this requires an equal tipping angle for each ski.

Once you have a rhythm going back and forth, add in the movements of flexing the inside leg and extending the outside leg. Through trial and error you'll learn the right amounts of each. Too much or too little will make you lose your balance. Practice on easy terrain so that speed control is not an issue. I use this exercise with all my students, as it's a safe way to learn more advanced carving and engagement at higher edge angles.

Creating Complete Rounded Arcs

I often see skiers who want to become experts, or to develop deep carving angles, desperately trying to produce body angles with forceful methods like leg extension. In their minds, they are pushing their bodies way inside the arc to get the high angles. Look back at Figure 3-11.

This approach mistakenly forgets about the need to balance with the edge angles, and it results in compensatory movements that reverse the progress toward expert skiing. When the new stance leg is extended vigorously at the beginning of an arc, in the High-C zone with the skis still pointed outward (at the target), the extension pushes your body downhill.

"Don't push yourself out of balance."

This vigorous extension is usually at the expense of balance — the body is pushed so far downhill that it is no longer in balance over the stance ski. If you're not balanced on the stance ski, then it's not going to create an arc and you'll be disconnected from your contact with the snow. This short-lived moment is followed by regaining balance on the inside ski, or by twisting the stance ski across the fall line to try to slow the body's descent.

Skiers achieve higher levels of performance when they balance on the stance ski and stay connected with it. The effort to increase edge and body angles should come from flexing and tipping with the inside leg, and the outside leg should only extend enough to keep that ski in contact with the snow.

The keys to a balanced, High-C turn entry are learning to tip and riding patiently in balance over the edges. Balance over the stance ski in the High-C zone is sufficient to engage the edge and start a groove. There is no need to push on the ski and make it dig into the snow. Once the skis have arced into the fall line, the stance leg should be almost fully extended to take the upcoming load. Through the bottom of the turn the arc will create the sensation of pressure, and you'll need to be strong in the stance leg to keep it extended and carve a solid arc. You'll need to stabilize the muscles of the hips and torso against this load, too. However, there should still be no effort to push your body away from the ski.

This book is written to help skiers develop the fundamental movements of skiing right from the beginning. Flexing and extending with the right intent and at the right time will let you tap into the energy available in linked turns. This reduces the physical stresses of inefficient skiing. Using energy from one turn to help with the transition to the next provides more control over turns and speed, with less fatigue. One of the major breakthroughs in skiing comes from flexing your legs.

The Ground Pushes Back in Expert Turns

Skiers who do develop and store energy through the turn often tell me that they feel the ground pushing back into their bodies. They are feeling the pressure that the forces of the arc are exerting on the body, specifically through the legs into the torso. Pressure through the body develops when the ski is angled and bent against the fall line, so the ski has to conform to a shortening, sharper arc than in passive side cut arcs. The extended outside leg holds, not yielding to the building pressure, and tips to greater angles due to the continued flexing and tipping of the inside leg.

Once you develop and sense this pressure from the ski into the body, you can release and redirect it to make it move your body over the skis into the next arc. You control it by flexing the legs and hinging the skis off the old edges at the time of release. This makes you exit the turn, and it takes the bend out of the skis. In transition, the energy from the bent ski is held by the muscles of the legs and torso. While your muscles are storing the energy from the previous turn, your skis are floating over the surface.

Figure 3-20. *Tip to the new edges with both legs flexed, as in the darkened frames.*

Floating

In *Anyone Can Be an Expert Skier 2*, I introduced the concept of floating between turns. This and the previous photomontage demonstrate transitions with float. In the transition, the legs are equally bent and the skis are close to or actually flat on the snow for a brief moment.

Figure 3-21. *The float makes it easy to tip. Flexing quickly as in Frames 3–4 makes the skis light for easy tipping.*

When you first observe the darkened frames in Figure 3-20, and Frames 3–4 in Figure 3-21, they might appear to be a strenuous, physically demanding period. That's where the analysis of skiing can be incorrect.

When coaches or skiers analyze skiing photos they can only interpret what they see based on their personal experience. Here, since I am the skier in the photos, I can convey to you what is actually happening to me and what

I am doing to create movement and actions. It is very difficult for a coach or instructor who has never performed a quality movement to convey such a movement accurately. In my view, this is why we have so much misunderstanding in ski instruction. Here, I am not relying on second hand interpretation, this is first hand.

In Figure 3-20, in the darker frames, it appears that I am fully exerting my muscles to keep from sitting or falling back. This is the float part of a turn. It may appear that my legs are working tremendously hard to stay in that low position, but actually I am floating. There is very little pressure on my skis and I am not trying to resist arcing loads or gravity. So, I am using little strength to hold that position. Also, I am not really holding a position, I am moving through to the new edges. When the legs bend to release, as in the darker frames, I am no longer resisting the turning forces and my skis exert little pressure on the snow. With the skis floating and light on the surface, I can tip the skis easily to their new angles for the next turn.

For a moment, think about what occurs if you use the opposite movement pattern to start a new turn, the traditional up-down pattern. Extension puts pressure on the skis. It is difficult to tip the skis when they are being pressed into the snow by an "up" extension. This is just one component that interrupts the transition and delays the edge engagement when using traditional up-down movements.

Another reason why analyzing skiing with photos can be misleading or incorrect is that photos are a static representation of a dynamic activity. You can stare at the shaded frames for a long time, and I'll appear to be holding that position for the whole time that you look at it. Certainly if I had to crouch in one of those positions and hold it for a minute, I would find it somewhat tiring. When I'm skiing, I don't try to hold myself in the position of any one photo frame — I move through them. Both sequences were photographed at 7.5 frames per second. Each frame lasts only 0.13 seconds. I hope my legs don't get tired if I bend them for half a second!

"Tip with the feet after active flexing; this makes the skis feel light on the surface, and helps keep your body in balance."

Creating Angles

Figure 3-22. *Create angles through flexion and balance.*

In Frames 1&2, my body is being pulled toward the fall line because I'm not resisting the release — my momentum is taking me there. Notice Frame 6, how complete and round the arc is and how far the arc is completed before flexing for release is initiated.

I don't need to push my body in the direction of the fall line or the new turn, nor do I want to. Pushing my body toward the fall line or letting myself fall down the mountain are very scary concepts to me and I never start turns

with that idea. I call the early, upper part of a turn (Frame 1) the High-C arc or being upside down to the slope. If you've never used energy from a previous turn to transition, this may appear to be a daunting position. The technique is attainable using the exercises in this book.

A High-C turn is achieved by transitioning with leg bending and knee flexing of the new inside leg. It gives skiers high levels of security on all slopes. Controlling the transition becomes easy as you become familiar with flexing and bending, which give the feeling of being suspended between turns. As you learn bending movements, you become aware of how easy it is to manage your speed and rate of transition. The more quickly you bend the old stance leg, the faster your body moves downhill and the sooner you get to the new edges; the more slowly you bend, the slower the transition. If I am moving too quickly to the next turn (going to the upside-down High-C phase) I slow the flexing or bending of the old stance leg and this slows the transition. If I want to speed up the transition, I flex the old stance leg more quickly and dynamically.

"Pressuring from ski to ski is done by flexing and extending, not by pushing the body from side to side."

Flexing the Legs Independently to Develop Angles

Novice and intermediate skiers typically flex and extend their legs in unison through turns and transitions. This keeps lean angles to a minimum. As skiers improve their tipping ability, hinging, they will increase their lean angles. However, tipping will only increase the angles so far unless the inside leg bends more than the outside as in Frame 4.

The inside leg must bend more to allow the hips to move laterally over the skis, into the center of the turn, creating a more acute angle of the legs to the snow. If the free-foot leg does

Figure 3-23. *Bend only the inside leg, so that it is shorter or more flexed than the stance leg, to develop steeper edge angles.*

not bend soon enough, or sufficiently, the body will lean onto it. Once the inside leg becomes a support for balance, it prevents the lean angle from increasing. In this case the inside leg is in the way.

Intermediate skiers who use a wide, two-footed stance rarely achieve highly inclined body angles, because their inside leg is providing too much support. The body cannot achieve higher edge angles, and there is not enough pressure on the outside ski to bend it into an arc.

If you have photos or videos of yourself skiing, compare them to the photos in this book to evaluate how much flexing of the inside leg you use compared to me.

Hans Grugger of the Austrian National Ski Team uses flexion of the inside leg and balance on the outside ski to reach maximum edge angles.

Transferring Weight or Pressure from Foot to Foot and Ski to Ski

As you develop the basics which enable you to ski with balance — the underlying premise of the *Anyone Can Be an Expert Skier 1 & 2* books — you'll be ready to adjust pressure from foot to foot, not only in transition, but also through turns. Transferring pressure from one foot to the other can be done completely, by lifting one ski completely off the snow, or it can be done gradually and progressively, by slowly flexing the new free leg.

Figure 3-24-B. *Through the arc. How much pressure is on the inside (right) foot and ski?*

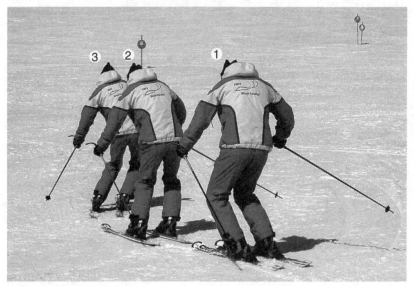

Figure 3-24-A. *Starting the arc. How much pressure is on the inside (right) foot and ski?*

Clearly, the Phantom Move (the "lift and tilt") provides an immediate, complete transfer of pressure to the new stance foot. Skiers should have full command of complete pressure transfers before they learn progressive or partial transfers. The results of not knowing the complete balance transfer are obvious in most skiers on the hill: they are unaware of where they stand and how to balance, therefore they make sloppy turns without grip that do not control speed or direction. If you aren't able to achieve complete balance on the outside ski, then you will not be in control of your balance from foot to foot. You're just getting what the hill and turn provide.

Before you start to vary the amount of pressure or weight on the inside ski in arcs, make sure that you can balance 100% on the outside ski. You can confirm this by lifting your inside ski (the free foot) in any arc. You should be able to continue slicing with the stance ski in its groove while you hold the free ski off the snow.

Flex to Pull Your Body into Angles, Not to Pull Your Foot Up

The Phantom Move lets you practice the movements that will soon be pulling your body into deep edge angles — combined tipping toward the little-toe edge and flexing (bending) the leg. However, as long as the movements pull your foot up toward your body, they will have less than complete influence on developing body angles.

In the next series of exercises, you'll take the movements of the Phantom Move — tipping and flexing — but keep the free foot engaged in the snow on its little-toe edge. Once again we treat the ski edge in its groove like a door that cannot pull away from its hinge. In this case, your tipping and flexing will pull your body into the arc, toward the snow, as opposed to pulling the foot away from the snow, up to you.

When you first attempt to use some inside foot pressure in your turns, any limitations in balancing will be evident. Typically, skiers lean too much on the inside leg. It's important to vary the pressure on the inside ski through tipping, flexing, and extending with the inside foot and leg, not by leaning the torso in that direction. Adjust pressure and create angles with the feet and legs, not with the shoulders or torso.

Tip the Free Foot without Lifting to Begin Engagement

Figure 3-25. *Start your practice by tipping the inside ski in a traverse. Keep the upper body steady over the stance ski.*

Your first few attempts at this exercise should be like a cat testing water with its paw. Cats are cautious about the unknown. They'll dip their paw just a little rather than jumping right in. This is good advice for this exercise. If you jump right in, committing too far uphill with your upper body, you might end up on your side on the snow. The inside ski can grab very quickly if the torso leans too much toward the inside ski as it is pressured and tipped.

Start on a moderate hill. Sliding in a traverse, tip the uphill ski further onto its little-toe edge. Keep enough weight on the ski that it tracks in a groove. Tip it enough that your inside knee tilts uphill from the ski. Once the ski grips and pulls uphill, reduce the tipping efforts without releasing the ski from its edge.

This exercise has two emphases. First, you have to be able to engage the uphill ski on its little-toe edge. It sounds like this is all tipping, but the leg needs to flex (bend) in order to let the shin and boot tilt up the hill. When done with some weight on the ski, I call this "side loading." Second, you have to be able to shift balance from one foot to the other, to manage the pressure on the uphill ski without leaning on it.

Side loading the inside ski connects your body to the snow with your tipping and flexing, so that your efforts will pull you into body angles. Side loading conveys to you where the pressure will be felt with the inside (free) foot: more on the side of the foot, less underneath the foot. Make the groove in the snow with the side edge, not the base edge.

Side Loading

Figure 3-26. *Side loading and flexing lead to higher edge angles.*

Focusing on leaving a groove in the snow with the side edge, rather than the base edge, will help you to achieve higher edge angles.

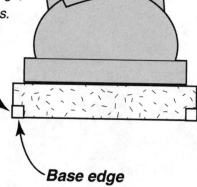

Side edge

Base edge

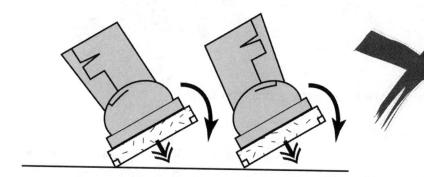

Extending too early in a turn can flatten the skis; the downward pressure tends to reduce the ski edge angle.

Flexing the inside leg reduces pressure on the ski for easy tipping. Putting pressure on the side edge encourages hinging.

Figure 3-27. *Example of free foot side loading, tipping, and releasing.*

In free skiing, you should avoid being overly committed to the inside ski. Overly committed means that you depend on that foot for balance. At any point in the turn, even when side loading, you should be able to lift the free ski off the snow.

For many skiers, the thought of "pressuring" the inside ski often shifts balance or weight to that foot without tipping it further, even making the ski flatten. The concept of side loading helps you to tip further to pull the body into deeper angles. Side loading is simply putting pressure onto the sidewall and side edge of the ski. To side load a ski requires that you tip the foot, boot, and leg to an angle, and that you keep the sidecut of the inside ski engaged. Side loading will activate the external rotator muscles of the inside leg. Don't mistakenly let this draw your feet into a wider stance. A wider stance will require that you support yourself with the inside foot, limiting tipping. When you bend your inside leg while side loading that ski, you develop the potential for higher edge angles, which make for better edge hold and carving.

Power Releasing

Power Releasing is an advanced exercise series that builds on side loading in a traverse to bring these angles into linked turns. It is physically strenuous, and will require your full range of flexion, so make sure you warm up with several vigorous runs and stretch before you start on these exercises.

One of the challenges of the series is that the exercises should be performed on a steep groomed slope. It requires the speed and the pitch to keep your balance over the stance ski.

The exercises are just not effective at slow speeds on a gentle pitch.

Foot separation is a key to this exercise series. The Power Release develops comfort in separating your feet vertically, not horizontally — this requires the steeper slope.

What are the signs of vertical separation? With vertical separation the legs are close together, and the inside boot is close, often even touching the extended stance leg.

H is horizontal separation: how wide my feet are apart. Even at these high edge angles, H is about hip width apart, no different than if I were standing on a flat hill without moving.

V is vertical separation. If I were standing on a flat hill and picked one foot straight up under my hip, the height I lifted it would be V. The more V you achieve through flexing the inside leg, the steeper an edge angle you can achieve.

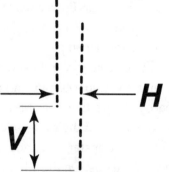

Figure 3-28. *Horizontal and vertical separation of the feet.*

Figure 3-29. *In Frames 3, 4, & 5 my skis are at least 2 feet apart. Yet my inside ski boot is touching the extended outside leg. This is vertical separation. It bends the outside ski and produces balance, high edge angles, speed control and huge edge grip. A wide stance with space between the thighs and knees does not produce the same balance, grip, or arc.*

If you have read any of my previous books, you'll probably be amazed at what you are reading: "Harald wants me to ski with a wide stance???" Okay, let's not get carried away. This wide stance is specific to the exercises here; it's not an everyday, every turn skiing stance. In the context of the Power Release, the wide stance lets you learn and exaggerate the long leg/short leg relationship of vertical separation. Skiers who have energy in linked arcs at faster speeds and on steeper terrain can justify a certain space between their feet, because the additional momentum at their release ensures a decisive balance transfer and movement of the body across the skis. On the other hand, a wide stance is a limitation for novice and intermedi-

ate skiers. With their slower speeds and shallower edge angles, they lack the momentum at transition needed to transfer balance and move the body across the wider stance. They will get stuck in transition standing on two feet. That limitation is exactly the reason for the vigorous extension taught in traditional technique.

In the case of the Power Release, we'll start each exercise with the wide stance. Once you are up to speed with sufficient tipping and side loading, the width of the stance will transform into vertical separation with a functional stance width. Plus, the flexion of the stance leg at the bottom of each arc actually brings the skis back to a narrower stance in time for transition (see Fig. 3-35, Frames 1–4).

Figure 3-30. *Wide Stance Traverse — separate skis at the beginning of the traverse.*

WIDE STANCE TRAVERSE

Start in a traverse at about 45 degrees to the fall line. Side load the uphill ski. As you pick up some speed, increase the tipping of the skis and the separation between the skis. To separate the skis, bend the inside leg while keeping the outside leg extended. Bend the inside leg so far that you have your knee tucked up against your chest.

The objective is to tip and bend together while maintaining balance on the stance ski (with the extended leg). This will make the skis carve an arc, shooting you back up the hill like a slingshot. This uphill trajectory will slow you down. As the skis head uphill, gradually bend your stance leg (previously extended) while keeping the skis on edge. This will reduce the separation between the skis, and you'll finish with both legs flexed and the skis side by side on edge. *Do not extend the uphill leg to finish —*

flex the old stance leg until it matches the bend of the inside leg.

Like all exercises, you'll improve your performance with practice. On your first attempts, you might find that your weight settles onto the inside, flexed leg. This indicates too little speed and too little tipping. Your comfort with the movements and trust in the results will come.

This exercise is not beyond the reach of intermediate skiers, even if the hill is steeper than where you normally ski in comfort. If you can find an isolated steep pitch, that's perfect. Simply perform the exercise all the way down until you are beyond the pitch, then resume skiing. You can perform single Wide Stance Traverses to a stop, and not have to link turns on the steep pitch.

A STEEPER BEGINNING

After practicing the exercise beginning from a moderate angle to the slope, increase your starting angle by pointing more downhill. This will give you more speed at the beginning. Higher speed means higher angles are possible!

Figure 3-31. *Wide Stance Traverse — a steeper beginning creates more speed.*

Frame 1. *Start in a relaxed wide stance in the fall line.*
Frame 3. *Lower your body by bending the inside leg; side load the inside ski.*

Frames 4–5. *Continue to bend and tip the inside leg and keep the outside leg extended until the skis begin to climb back uphill.*

With more speed you'll pull some G-forces through the bottom of the arc, as the skis head across the fall line. Though it's still a traverse, this version of the exercise mimics the loads of carved turns. Try to feel the weight shift onto the outside, extended stance leg as the skis start to bite and bring the arc back uphill. Try to create this weight shift earlier in the turn by coordinated tipping and bending of the inside leg.

Once you have the load built up on the outside ski, you can bend that leg starting at the bottom of the arc to let the stance ski carve back up next to the free ski.

In free skiing, use the same extend/flex relationship as in Frame 5, but with a functional, narrower stance. The stance can become narrower as flexing the inside leg becomes more habitual.

Figure 3-32. *Wide Stance Traverse — as the arc carves uphill, flex the stance leg until it matches the flex of the inside leg. This is preparation for the release.*

Notice in the last three frames that my outside leg begins to bend or flex. As I flex the stance leg, the skis come together. This is the precursor to the release for the next arc. The idea is to keep the momentum through the arc, and flex in preparation for the release into the next arc.

Linked Power Releases

When you can perform solid Wide Stance Traverses in both directions, you'll be ready to take the energy and momentum from one directly into a release. This is the Power Release. Make sure that you flex the stance leg through the bottom of the arc to bring the skis back together. When both legs are flexed, tip (don't twist or turn) the skis to the new edges. Engage the edges and balance over them, just like in the tipping exercises in the previous chapter.

LONG LEG/SHORT LEG THROUGH TURN

Figure 3-33. *After the release, as you tip the skis to the new edges, begin to separate the skis in the upper third of the arc and flex the inside leg as much as you can. Then proceed as in the Wide Stance Traverses to prepare for the release.*

WHEN DO WE FLEX WITHOUT RELEASING?

The last frame in Figure 3-33 demonstrates a tightening of the turn arc. It also shows the stance leg more flexed (bent) than in the previous frame, yet the skis are not yet flattening for release. When the outside leg is fully extended, you are at the limit of edge and body angles. In order to increase those angles to tighten the turn arc, you'll need to flex the stance leg (just a little). Think of this flexing as giving in slightly to the pressure of the arc. This will enable you to tip the boots and skis to a slightly higher edge angle.

Be prepared at the moment you flex and increase tipping. The arc will tighten, increasing the pressure you feel under the arcing skis.

The Power Release has multiple benefits. You'll practice flexing and tipping together, learn to arc with balance over the stance ski at high edge angles, work the legs independently, create arcing loads, and achieve an energetic release.

Figure 3-34. *Power Release in linked turns. Above, actual frame locations. Below, expanded for clarity.*

Frame 1. *I'm flexed at release. The outside ski and leg match the inside ski and leg.*
Frame 2. *Tip the inside leg and perform extreme flexion. Make sure you are side loading the free ski. This will drop your inside hip toward the inside of the turn.*
Frame 3. *Extend the outside leg. The bent ski shows where pressure is concentrated.*

Frame 4. *Balance on outside ski.*
Frames 5–6. *Through the Lower-C part of the arc, flex (bend) the outside leg while increasing tipping of both skis. This will make the outside ski arc up toward the inside ski, matching the skis.*

Frame 1. *This is a high-angle, powerful carving turn with extreme flex of the inside leg.*

Frame 2. *Keep the stance leg extended into the Lower-C arc.*

Frame 3. *Bend the outside, stance leg to let the stance ski arc back up beside the inside ski. This is the start of the Power Release.*

Frame 4. *In the Power Release, with extreme flexing and tipping. Only tip — no twisting!*

Frame 5. *Tip the new free ski (previous stance ski) first to engage the skis in the High-C arc.*

Frame 6. *The objective for the middle of the turn arc is to experience the flexing range of the inside leg and the extension range of the outside leg.*

Figure 3-35. *Power Release through transition in linked turns.*

The Power Release exercise sequence expands your range of flexing and extending, and creates high edge angles. It helps you make changes in days of practice that would take years to develop simply in free skiing. It makes you aware of what it takes to make a leap to the next level of skiing performance.

Through the exercises in this chapter, you should have increased your range of flexing and extending, learned the correct timing of each action to create smooth releases and strong engagement, and learned how to flex the legs independently to increase edge angles and tighten your turn radius. If you feel that the exercises are beyond your capabilities, or if you need verification of your performance, come to a Harb Ski Camp suitable for your level of skiing.

When you combine the flexing abilities learned in this chapter to the tipping you learned in the previous chapter, your feet and legs are ready to take you skiing wherever you wish to go. These movements are essentials. You can simply keep practicing them in order to improve.

Right now, you are ready to add some movements of the upper body to complement your new lower-body actions. By complement, I mean to take advantage of the lower-body movements and make them more effective. I have mentioned both counterbalancing and counteracting movements on several occasions throughout this and the last chapter. The next chapter deals with counterbalancing in earnest.

Marco Buechel of the Liechtenstein National Ski Team demonstrates extreme flexion of the inside leg. His high edge angles are achieved with vertical separation of the feet, not horizontal.

CHAPTER 4

Essential — Counterbalancing

C OUNTERBALANCING IS SIDE-TO-SIDE TILTING OF THE UPPER BODY at the waist or belt line. It should be performed at the same time, but in the opposite direction, of any tipping of the feet. Counterbalancing movements for an upcoming turn need to start while you are still on the previous edges, as you are starting to flatten the skis. If you wait until you are on your new edges before you counterbalance, it's too late.

Figure 4-1. *Counterbalancing through transition.*

Counterbalancing

In Figure 4-1, Frame 5, the downhill hand (closer to the bottom of the mountain; here, the right) is lifted higher than the uphill hand (here, the left). This relationship of the hands indicates the strong counterbalancing movements required for balancing in the High-C arc. However, the counterbalancing movements that tipped the torso and created the difference in the level of the hands began in Frame 2.

Most skiers do not separate the movement of their upper body, especially lateral tilting or leaning, from the movements of their feet. When the feet tip to the right, the shoulders and torso also lean to the right. This creates total body lean, which reduces edge grip and balance on the edges. Many shaped skis provide good grip even when the body is leaned to the inside of the arc. However, if you become overly dependent on the skis to create the grip and are lazy with the upper body, eventually there will be a ceiling to your performance.

"The more you challenge your balance, the more it improves."

Leaning the body inside the turn is fine if you want to cruise along on easy or moderate slopes, and not worry about the steep or icy sections where everyone slips and slides. I hear it all the time, "I can ski fine up here, but when it gets steep or icy I can't control my speed." Lack of counterbalancing is a likely reason for those problems. For skis to hold really well on steeps, a skier has to use counterbalancing movements.

Even advanced recreational skiers and junior racers lack counterbalancing movements, either because they haven't been taught those movements or because they neglect to use them when needed. If you don't practice counterbalancing regularly, even on slopes where you "don't need it," then it won't be part of your repertoire on the harder slopes where you do need it.

If you watch Giorgio Rocca, Daron Rahlves, or Benni Raich — some of the best racers in the world — they know how to ski on easy terrain, they know how to ski on steep terrain where sharp turns are needed, and they know how to ski when it's icy and the course is rough. This versatility comes from implementing good technique at all times.

If you watch the greatest tennis player in the world, and possibly of all times, Roger Federer, you'll see that he has the complete game. He doesn't have a weak backhand volley, or a weak crosscourt approach shot, or any other weak spot — his whole game, all the shots, are strong. A good skier should be the same — solid in all aspects of performance. If you know that you'll need good counterbalancing when you hit the steep and icy slopes, or bumps and short turns, why ski with weak counterbalancing movements? Knowing and using all the essentials gives the skier the complete game. Few skiers have this game until they start using Primary Movements Teaching System technique.

Counterbalancing Is Stealthy

Many skiers have difficulty comprehending the degree of effort required within the torso to achieve sufficient counterbalancing. If you look at the montage on the following pages, you can see that the torso does not move much from one turn to the other. Many skiers comment to me that it looks like my body just stays "still" when I ski. Unfortunately, this lack of apparent movement of the torso leads some skiers to believe that no effort is required within the torso. If the body's not moving, then there's no effort there, right?

Wrong! If I did not have counteracting movements within my torso during my linked arcs, my body would lean back and forth with my head and shoulders in the center of the arc. The effort of counterbalancing alternates from one side of my torso to the other, opposite the actions of the feet. It is only through this alternating internal effort that I achieve the look of the steady torso and the performance of counterbalancing.

Kurt Engl, an Austrian World Cup racer, doesn't get these angles by accident; he's counterbalancing.

Figure 4-2. *Counterbalancing highlighted in the Sample Turn (left and right; stretched).*

Through the arc of the turn, counterbalancing efforts result in an angle between the torso and the legs. One easy way to observe this angle is to look at the zipper on the front of a skier's jacket and compare it with the line of the legs. In the middle and lower portions of the arc, if this angle is 150 degrees or less, the skier is using counterbalancing.

Frame 1. *The angle is less than 150 degrees. This is a result of counterbalancing.*

Frame 5. *As the skis come flat in transition, the angle opens to 180 degrees. We call this neutral. However, there is still tension within the muscles of the torso to control the body over the legs. The skis are tipping to the left, through flat, therefore my torso effort is to tip to the right.*

Frames 6–9. *As the skis are tipped to a higher edge angle, the angle of torso to legs increases, making the counterbalancing efforts apparent.*

Frame 5. *Neutral in transition.*

Frame 1. *Counterbalancing creates the angle between the legs and the torso.*

Coordinate Tipping and Counterbalancing

If you are tipping your skis to the right, your legs will also move to the right following the tipping action of the skis. If you move the upper body right, the same direction as the skis and legs, you will fall in that direction.

In transition, the skis are changing edges.

Though they do not have much edge angle through transition, they are being tipped. Counterbalancing movements are performed to counter the tipping actions, not the edge angle. Just as the feet tip through transition, so should the body counterbalance.

Frame 5. *The torso is angled to the legs, above the fall line.*

Figure 4-3. *It is necessary to move the upper body to counteract the shift of lower body mass and its developing momentum.*

Feel and Strengthen Your Counterbalancing Movements

SIDE CRUNCH EXERCISE

To sense the muscle contractions of counterbalancing, and to train and strengthen those muscles, you can perform side crunches. I use a Roman Bench to perform side crunches. If you don't have access to workout facilities, you can do these at home on a sofa with a partner. Place your hip on a padded sofa arm, with your feet on the sofa cushions, and your torso extending off the end of the sofa. Have your partner hold your feet and legs solidly on the sofa cushions so that you can crunch your torso without your legs lifting up.

Start by holding your body aligned with your legs — do not sag with the torso. If you have been avoiding your core workouts, you'll know it now. If you find it easy to hold your torso steady then try a crunch: tighten the muscles on the side of your torso that you are *not* lying on (here, my right) as though to bring your rib cage closer to your hip bone. This should lift your shoulders and head away from the floor. Lower yourself until your legs and spine are in a straight line, and repeat. For the toughest version, lower your torso to bring your head and shoulders closer to the floor to start, then crunch up. Repeat.

Figure 4-4. *The side crunch on a Roman Bench will strengthen the muscles that perform counterbalancing. This will improve your ability to ski with high edge angles.*

STATIONARY TIPPING WITH A FOCUS ON COUNTERBALANCING

Practice again the dryland tipping exercises, on the flat and across the fall line (Figures 2-1 and 2-2), as well as stationary edge changes on snow on a flat area (Figure 2-6). Focus now on tipping the torso opposite the direction that the feet tip. If you can observe yourself in a mirror while tipping on the carpeted ramp, see that your torso leans opposite the direction that you tip your feet. Put on a top or jacket with a zipper down the front if you need a visual reference.

As you do these exercises again, start by focusing on your feet. The boots should stay parallel, and, in the exercises with skis, both skis must tip to the same edge angle. Just as before, make sure you tip the skis in their tracks, with no twisting or slipping especially when the skis are flat. Accurate tipping movements with the feet are the basis for the counterbalancing of the upper body.

Once your feet are tipping well, lean the torso opposite to the direction of the tipping. When you tip to your limit, crunch the side muscles in the torso and hold them flexed. If your feet are tipped as far to the right as possible, your left side muscles should be squeezing your left ribs against your left hip bone. This simulates the effort that will actually be required once you are skiing.

Two ingredients that build success in skiing are tipping with the feet and counterbalancing with the torso. Together they help you to balance on the edges of your skis while you are sliding. Rehearse these movements in dryland training, then in stationary exercises, so that they will be standard parts of your skiing repertoire. You'll be rewarded once you are arcing on snow.

Figure 4-5. *Practice dryland tipping again, adding the focus on your counterbalancing movements. The zig-zag line in the images indicates the side of the torso that crunches in order to pull the ribs toward the hip bone.*

Stationary Tipping on a Side Hill

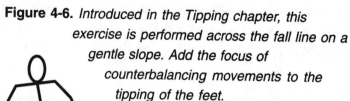

Figure 4-6. *Introduced in the Tipping chapter, this exercise is performed across the fall line on a gentle slope. Add the focus of counterbalancing movements to the tipping of the feet.*

Frame 1. *Start with the legs slightly flexed and the feet tipped slightly uphill (here, the left). Counterbalancing effort is opposite to tipping, so tip the torso to the right. Tighten the muscles that hold your right ribs against your hip bone.*

Frame 2. *The neutral position at transition is achieved by tipping the feet downhill (to the right), to flatten the skis, and tipping the torso uphill (to the left), opposite the feet.*

Frame 3. *Keep tipping the skis downhill and leaning the torso uphill until you are balanced on the new High-C edges. Balance for a moment in this position, and tighten the muscles on the uphill side of the torso.*

The Pole Lean

As in the previous chapter, exaggeration when practicing is useful for learning the new movements. You can experience the counterbalancing movements necessary at high edge angles by leaning against a sturdy pole, wall, or other solid item.

Figure 4-7-A. *Tip the feet until you lean your hip against the pole. Keep the torso vertical.*

Frame 1. *Stand about two feet away from the pole, with the skis tipped on edge toward the pole. Because you are balanced on edge, you need just enough counterbalancing to stand up. Tip the feet to a higher edge angle to bring your hips toward the pole.*

Frame 2. *Keep tipping the feet until you lean against the pole with your hip. Make sure that you lean against the pole with your hip first, not with your shoulders. Once you are leaning, keep the torso vertical. Tighten the muscles on the side of the torso that's not touching the pole. This holds the angle between the legs and torso.*

Figure 4-7-B. *Increase your edge and torso-to-leg angles first by stepping the feet away from the pole, then by flexing the legs.*

Frame 3. *Starting from Frame 2 on the opposite page, increase the edge angle of your legs by stepping the skis away from the base of the pole. Keep the skis on edge with each step so you don't slip. Notice that I am keeping my legs extended here. Keep the upper body vertical with the hip against the pole.*

Frame 4. *Flex both legs, keep tipping both skis on edge, and let your hip slide down the pole to achieve even greater edge angles. Keep the body upright. Experiencing the increase in edge angle enabled by flexing the legs is an important aspect of this exercise, as well as the counterbalancing. Look back at Figure 3-33 to see how a slight "pre-flex" before release enables higher edge angles and a tighter arc.*

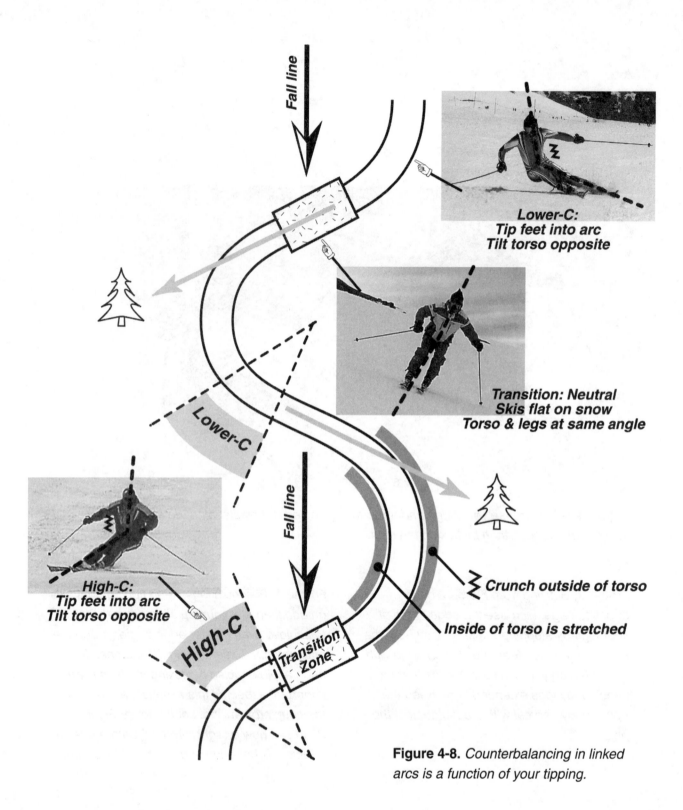

Fall line

Lower-C:
Tip feet into arc
Tilt torso opposite

Transition: Neutral
Skis flat on snow
Torso & legs at same angle

Lower-C

Fall line

High-C:
Tip feet into arc
Tilt torso opposite

High-C

Transition Zone

ⵏ **Crunch outside of torso**

Inside of torso is stretched

Figure 4-8. *Counterbalancing in linked arcs is a function of your tipping.*

Counterbalancing in Turns

After practicing the exercises up to here, you should know exactly where the muscles are that produce counterbalancing, and how to tighten them to tilt your torso opposite your feet. It's now time to apply this action in your ski turns.

To know where and when to perform your counterbalancing, you simply have to relate that to the tipping of your feet. Any time that the feet are tipping toward the right, tighten the muscles on the left side of your torso in order to lean the shoulders to the left. Remember, don't wait until the skis are on the new edges to begin counterbalancing; start the counterbalancing at the same time as the tipping. Pace your counteracting movements to match the feet. If you tip the feet slowly, tilt the torso slowly; if you tip the feet quickly, tilt the torso quickly.

EXAGGERATED IN CARVED ARCS

To begin counterbalancing in turns, start with linked arcs on a flat slope. Tip the skis to the new edges and leave two clean grooves in the snow. Crunch the ribs against the hip bone on the outside of the arc. Here, my feet tip right, my torso tilts left, so the crunching effort is on the left side.

Figure 4-9. *As you tip to the new edges, exaggerate the crunch on the new stance side of the torso (here, the left).*

REACH FOR THE BOOT

Let's add counterbalancing to real skiing on intermediate slopes. The exercise is to reach for the top buckle on the side of your boot with the stance side (outside) hand, alternating the touch from side to side. The hands are not just flapping around on their own; the arms should be pulling the torso into strong counterbalancing. The hand that reaches for the boot top lowers the shoulder and arm, pulls the torso to the side, and indicates the side where you'll crunch the ribs toward the hip bone. If you are flexible enough to touch the boot buckle, great. Otherwise, touch the outside of the stance knee. The objective is to tilt the torso, not to touch the boot.

Figure 4-10-A. *Through the end of the previous arc.*

Frame 1. *The torso is angled to the legs.*

Frame 1. *At the end of the previous turn (or if you start from a traverse), the arm on the downhill side is touching the knee while the uphill arm is lifted to shoulder height. Notice that the torso is angled to the legs, thus the arm action has had the desired influence on the torso.*

Frames 2–3. *As you start to flatten the skis for release, the counterbalancing effort also shifts. Use the hands to guide your torso; start to lift the downhill arm away from the knee.*

Figure 4-10-B.
Transition.

Frames 4–9. *This is the transition. Tip the skis from the old edges to the new and tilt the torso opposite the feet. Lift the new inside arm to shoulder height and reach the new stance arm to touch the knee.*

Figure 4-10-C. *High-C through middle of arc.*

Frame 10. *The inside arm is extended at shoulder height, while the outside arm is touching the side of the knee. Notice that the outside hand is still the* uphill *hand. I am on edge and counterbalanced above the fall line: High-C angles.*

Frames 11–12. *Through the Lower-C portion of the arc, continue to reach the outside hand toward the stance boot. Augment this reaching effort by crunching with that side of your torso.*

The Hip-O-Meter

The Hip-O-Meter is our name for attaching your ski poles across your hips so that they stick out on both sides. You'll see more of these exercises in Chapter 5, Counteracting.

Hip-O-Meter exercises have several benefits. First, by taking the poles out of your hands, you cannot lean on them for balance. You must balance only on your edges. Second, they create awareness of the orientation and movements of the hips. Unless you are a hula-hoop expert or a belly dancer, you probably don't have good awareness of what your hips and torso are doing at any time. With the Hip-O-Meter firmly strapped to the hips, the poles give you visual and tactile feedback about your pelvis so that you can learn to control this important part of your body.

There are several ways to attach your poles. If you have long straps, loop one strap over the basket of the other pole. Place one pole behind you and one in front, and slip the other strap over the basket. If you do not have pole straps, or if they are not long enough, use supersized elastic bands or small bungee cords. Make sure that the front pole is sitting across the front of your hip bones, not above them on your waist. When you start to practice with the Hip-O-Meter on snow, choose easy terrain where you aren't likely to fall.

INDOOR HIP-O-METER PRACTICE

Strap on your poles, buckle your boots, and stand on your carpeted ramp in front of a mirror. See if you can tip the poles (so that one end points slightly toward the ground) by tipping your hips, letting the legs flex and extend slightly. Try to turn your pelvis so that one end of the poles aims slightly forward, the other backward. Do this without your shoulders turning. (That's practice of counteracting movements for the next chapter.)

Once you have experimented a little with the Hip-O-Meter, practice for the next, on-snow exercise. Start by tipping your boots to one side and tilting your torso in the opposite direction. Take the hand on your stance side — the same side as the torso crunch — and lightly set it on the pole ends. Press down slightly with that hand to encourage you to tip the feet and counterbalance to higher angles. Practice on both sides.

Figure 4-11. *Touching the hand on the outside end of the poles encourages higher foot-tipping and torso-tilting angles.*

Make linked, carved arcs with the Hip-O-Meter. Touch the outside hand to the pole tips, and keep the inside hand lifted above and slightly forward of the poles. Make sure that you focus on the essentials of tipping and flexing to create clean grooves in the snow. The counterbalancing movements should combine and coordinate with the tipping. As you transition from one arc to the next, make sure that you tip your feet and tilt your torso. The tilting of the torso opposite the feet will automatically switch your hands and arms for the new arc. Touch the ends of the poles with the stance hand to confirm that you have tipped the torso adequately.

If you can keep the poles level throughout the lined arcs, and through transition, you'll know that your counterbalancing efforts are sufficient and well timed. If the poles point toward the ground inside the arc of the skis, then you don't have enough counterbalancing.

Have someone watch you and give feedback, or take video, to ensure that you are doing this correctly. Skiers at our camps often reverse the hands (inside on pole ends, outside lifted) their first few tries.

Hip-Touch Turns

The next on-snow counterbalancing exercise will use your stance hand on the outside hip to encourage you to crunch harder on that side of your torso and create a greater torso-to-leg angle. You'll have no poles for this exercise — it challenges your balance and it keeps your hands free to touch and reach.

Figure 4-12. *Push the stance hand against the hip to encourage a stronger tilt at the waist. Keep the inside hand high and away from the body.*

Start on an easier hill than usual where you can think about when and what you are doing. Gradually work up to linking turns at your regular speed and pitch.

As soon as you tip your skis on edge, place the outside hand (stance side hand; side opposite the direction of tipping of the feet) on your hip bone and push that hip inward toward the center of the arc. Hold the other arm extended at shoulder height. In transition, as you tilt your skis through flat, bring both hands in front of you and touch them, simply to signify that the arms and torso are also going through neutral. Switch hands, pressing the new stance hand against that hip, just as you tip the skis onto their new edges. Pressing firmly with the stance (hip) hand while lifting with the inside arm creates strong counterbalancing movements of the torso. You might be surprised at the edge angles and grip you can develop with this exercise.

Implementing Counterbalancing in Your Skiing

Once you have had good success with these exercises, you'll want to bring the new movement pattern into "regular" free skiing. Sometimes, in the step from exercise to free skiing, some of the movements are diminished or lost.

Plan to make a few runs where you alternate between exercise turns and free skiing. For example, make 4 to 6 turns where you touch your knee on the outside of the turn (Figure 4-10), then make a few turns without touching the knee, but trying to keep the torso counterbalanced just as far, then back for another 4 to 6 turns with touching. With the Hip-Touch exercises, make a few turns where you push hard with the stance hand on the hip, then make a few turns with the hands in your regular pole-holding position. Alternate between the two types of turns until everything — ski edge angles, ski grip, counterbalancing effort, torso-to-leg angle — is the same, except the position of the hand on the hip.

Runs that combine exercise and free skiing will hasten the integration of the new movements into your skiing. That's how we build the complete game.

Monika Bergmann-Schmuderer of the German National Ski Team demonstrates counterbalancing through the Lower-C arc.

CHAPTER 5

Essential — Counteracting

COUNTERACTING MOVEMENTS ARE ROTATION OF THE TORSO AROUND THE SPINE, starting at the hips and lower back, and affecting the whole torso up through the shoulders. Counteracting movements are performed in the opposite direction to the passive following of the legs due to tipping the skis. If you tilt your skis onto their left edges, they will arc toward the left, eventually pointing left. The legs follow this tipping by turning to the left. The counteracting movement in this case is to turn the torso as though to face toward the right. Your effort is to turn the torso counter to, or opposite to, the direction that the skis will point.

What do counteracting movements do for us in skiing? They guarantee strong edge contact and strong engagement of the ski tails, they assist in counterbalancing, and they permit the skeletal stacking that reduces muscle fatigue. Counteracting movements give you more performance from your skis.

Let's take a look at the Sample Turn so that we can accurately describe the movements and results of counteracting through linked turns. Through the end of an arc, the Lower-C portion of the turn, the skis are on edge and arcing from the fall line until they point across the slope. As you can see in the Sample Turn and many other montages throughout the book, through this portion of the arc my hips and torso are at a slight angle to my skis, with my inside hip, shoulder, and arm slightly more forward. This visible angle between the torso and the skis can be called a "countered relationship"; it is the indicator of the efforts within my torso to counteract the tendency of my body to turn and face into the center of the arc. Look again at Figure 1-10.

Figure 5-1. *The Sample Turn with counteracting movements described.*

As I flex and tip to begin releasing the skis, the countered relationship remains until my skis reach flat. Once my skis are flat, the hips and shoulders should also be in neutral, as we have already seen in previous chapters. Neutral with respect to counteracting means that the body faces along the length of the skis. There is no angle between the two. For the brief moment of transition, my body moves through square.

My next move is to tip the skis onto their new edges. At this point, I will start to counter-act the tipping by facing my hips and torso slightly outside the upcoming arc. In the Sample Turn, the engagement shown starting in Frame 6 is onto the left edges, so I will turn my torso toward the right. The result of this internal effort is again a visible angle between my torso and skis: my inside arm, shoulder, and hips will be slightly forward of the stance side. At the top of the turn, these counteracting movements enhance edge hold as well as align me skeletally for the upcoming load of the arc.

Frame 1. *This frame shows the chest, front of jacket and zipper of jacket facing toward the stance ski.*

Frame 2. *The stance ski always has the outside edge off or lifted from the snow.*

Frame 3. *The countered upper body makes it possible to flex without losing ski angle.*

Frame 4. *The countered relationship moves to neutral as the skis start to come flat to the snow.*

Frame 5. *Skis flat, upper body neutral.*

Frames 6–9. *Upper body counter increases as edge angles increase. Body angles and ski grip are achieved with confidence if counteracting is happening.*

Why the Naysayers to Counteracting?

In American ski teaching circles, counteracting movements have lost favor over the last 20 years. Do I think this is detrimental to skiers and students? Yes! The lack of counteracting movements taught in traditional instruction is diminishing the skiing experience for thousands of skiers.

So why, despite their obvious benefits, have counteracting movements lost favor? It's mostly due to misunderstanding of what effective counteracting movements are, and as an overreaction to the potential negative results of using too much counteracting. Counteracting movements are like something from the story of Goldilocks and the three bears. You can have too much, too little, or an amount that's just right. The goal in PMTS technique is to teach you how to perform the movements and how to judge their sufficiency so that it's just right.

The naysayers to counteracting in traditional instruction typically cite the negatives of *excessive* counter. Counteracting should not be viewed as an effort to reach and hold a position. This is likely to lead to an abrupt transition from one position to the other, perhaps even making the skis twist in transition (you know by now that you don't want that!) The goal is not to crank your hips and shoulders into an extreme angle and hold them throughout the arc until it's time to crank in the other direction. This wastes energy and is uncoordinated with your tipping efforts. Instead, we'll strive

for a proportionality of counteracting. The harder and faster you tip the skis, the more you have to counteract that effort. Gentler tipping on gentler slopes requires less counteracting. Knowing how to use counteracting movements, and moving into and out of the countered relationship as needed from arc to arc, will give you powerful, fluid arcs.

Understand that counteracting lives on a spectrum. On one side is "rotation," in the middle is "square," and on the other side is "counteracting." Rotation is the opposite of counteracting. It's a deliberate effort to turn the torso to face into the arc of the turn. This is a source of turning energy, but it flattens the skis, twists them, makes them skid, and does not produce edge grip in an arc. Square is the very thin line that separates counteracting, with its edge grip, tail hold, and skeletal stacking, from rotation, with its tail skidding.

Most of the anti-counter establishment promotes skiing in a square stance. A square stance is not strong in edging, merely adequate. It's hard to find and hold. It only takes a tiny glitch to lose square, and losing it inevitably leads to rotation with its lack of performance. Counteracting works in tandem with counterbalancing, and helps to maintain it. A square position often raises the outside hip. This lets go of any counterbalancing you have, leaning the shoulders and hips into the turn, destroying your edge grip.

Can We Really Tip without Turning?

In skiing, there is one action that kills ski performance and limits the progress of many skiers. Traditional instruction does not want to face this reality, and thus does not address the problem. I don't shy away from the issue. PMTS technique teaches you how to deal with it so that you can improve and progress. With the movement understanding that you'll gain from reading this book, you'll know exactly why your edges lose grip and your skis skid, and you'll know how to change that.

The action that creates the problems is passive rotation that accompanies tipping the skis. Because of the way our legs are built and function, tipping the feet turns the thighs in the hip sockets. This causes the thighs to swing from side to side under the hips as you edge. The legs follow the skis as you tip them. For example, tipping the skis onto the left edges makes them arc to the left; the legs will turn to the left as they follow the skis. The faster you tip the feet, the faster the thighs will turn. Whether we like it or not, the essential action of tipping the feet has the unwanted byproduct of applying torque to the skis.

When your skis are already engaged on edge and you tip to a higher (or lower) edge angle, the rotation doesn't cause performance problems. It is easily managed. The performance issue arises at turn transition, when you are tipping from one set of edges, through flat, to the other edges. When the skis are flat or at low edge angles, the torque due to the rotation of the thighs will tend to turn or pivot the skis.

If the desire is for linked arcs without a skid, for gaining balance and grip early in the arc, and for achieving High-C angles, then the skis have to tip from edge to edge without direction change. To achieve this, the skier has to do something to manage or negate the twisting influence of the legs on the skis. This "something" is counteracting.

In PMTS technique, upper-body movements are not used to create energy to turn the skis. Counterbalancing and counteracting are used to stabilize the upper body, assist in reaching higher edge angles, and increase ski edge engagement. Counteracting movements specifically are intended to reduce the rotational input from the legs (due to tipping) to the skis, and to prevent the hips and upper body from accompanying the legs in their rotation.

In many of the photomontages in this book, the transition takes place in one to two frames. At 7.5 frames per second, this means that the edge change takes about one-quarter of a second. When you think of your thighs swinging from one side to the other in a quarter second, you realize that there's a lot of energy in that motion of the legs. The more dynamic the turn transition, the faster the legs swing from side to side, and the more energy there is that is trying to twist the skis. To become an expert skier, you need to know how to control this so that it doesn't twist your skis out from under you.

If the rotation of the thighs drags the hips and upper body into rotation, not only will the skis rotate, flatten, and skid, but the entire torso will continue to rotate in that direction through the entire turn. If the upper body is rotating in the direction of one turn, it makes it very difficult to go the other direction, and it requires an effort to stop the rotation of the whole body before you can go the other way.

Tipping the skis with the feet is the start of high-performance skiing. Learning to counteract in conjunction with tipping lets you derive the full benefit of edge grip and carving in your skiing.

WHY DO SKIERS USE THE UPPER BODY INCORRECTLY?

Traditional instruction de-emphasizes tipping the skis on edge. As a novice, if you do not learn to tip your feet, then there is no impetus for the skis to turn. It's apparent to most skiers on their first day on the slopes that the goal is to turn back and forth on the hill, or at least to face back and forth. If the skier is not learning to tip the skis with the feet, that means two things: 1. The skis will not turn on their own; 2. The skis will stay flat on the snow.

Since the skis are flat, they will not turn, so you need to do something to get around the corner. However, since the skis are flat, there's almost no resistance to pivoting or twisting. All it takes is a little turn of the shoulders or torso to face in the way you want to go — a little rotation — and the skis will turn and aim in that direction. If you're on a hill, once the skis turn to point across the slope, they will be slightly on edge, the resulting skid will slow you, and the skis will start to nudge you in the direction that you turned. Presto! You've made a ski turn!

Anytime thereafter that you feel the skis are not turning, you have the solution you learned on that first day: rotate the torso to face where you want to go, and the skis will pivot and follow. The more you practice this movement, the more it becomes your habit. Many traditional ski schools emphasize this movement pattern. If you've ever heard an instructor say, "Up and around," that student is learning to rise up to flatten the skis, then turn — not tip — in the new direction.

CHANGING YOUR HABIT OF ROTATING

This technique of rotating with the skis flat works for a while, until you decide that you really want to become a proficient skier. Perhaps you decide that you want to carve linked arcs or get higher edge angles.

The first step toward changing your performance is to master tipping. Until you learn to tip the skis on and off edge and to balance on them, you cannot simply cease your rotation or you will not turn. You need the new method in place before you can eliminate your habit.

Once you master tipping, the rotation habit becomes the enemy of performance. In order to derive the full benefits of tipping the skis, you have to learn a new movement pattern with your upper body — not only new, but opposite to your habit. That's where this chapter becomes helpful. The exercises here will help you to reverse your habit, to counteract instead of rotating at turn transition. Coordinating the counteracting movements from this chapter with the tipping you learned earlier, you'll be able to control the passive rotation of the legs and to avoid adding any other rotational input. Then you'll be skiing like an expert.

Learning Counteracting Movements

What are the keys to learning and using counteracting movements? As with the other essentials in the book, it's important for you to know where you are and where your skis are pointing relative to the turn and the hill. I'm going to explain counteracting movements based on your tipping movements, so review the tipping diagram if needed (Figure 2-33). Figure 5-2 is a new turn diagram, showing the timing of the counteracting movements.

Remember two things about PMTS technique. First, there are no frozen positions and no efforts that start, pause, or stop. Movements are done continuously. Tipping the skis back and forth should remind you of a metronome, ticking back and forth rhythmically. Counterbalancing movements pull you into and out of torso-to-leg angles. Counteracting will turn your torso from one countered relationship, through neutral, to the other side, and back again.

Second, the biggest changes in body relationship to the skis happen in transition, whether counterbalancing or counteracting. By comparison, the body changed little relative to the skis during the arc of the turn. Thus, if you get it right during the transition, you'll probably have it through the arc.

DIRECTION, NOT DISTANCE, OF MOVEMENT

The importance of movements like counterbalancing and counteracting is in the direction. Moving just one millimeter in the right direction (countering) will have a dramatically different effect on your skiing than moving just one millimeter in the wrong direction (rotation).

Monika Bergmann-Schmuderer of the German National Ski Team demonstrates counteracting — her torso is "facing the bases."

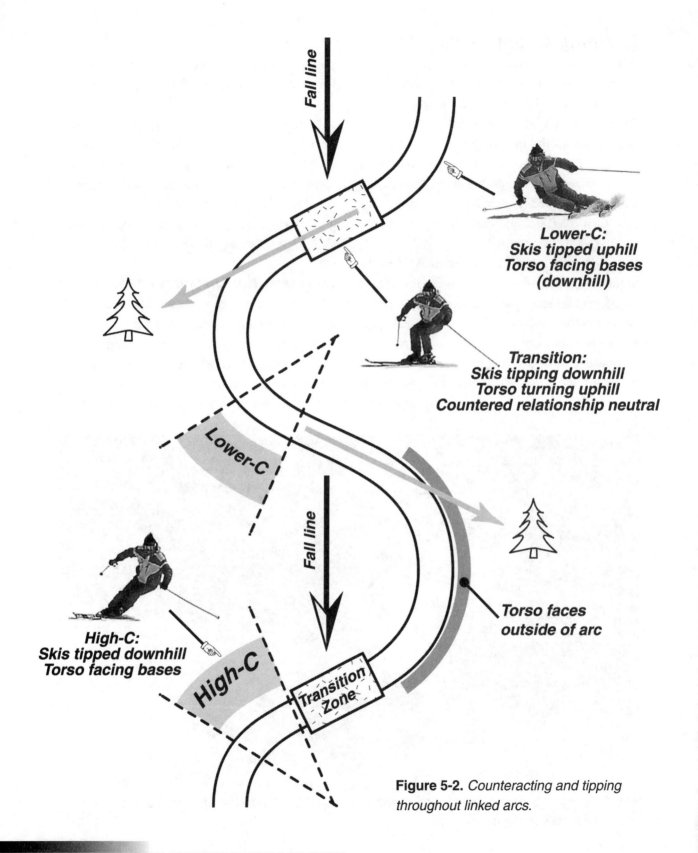

Fall line

Lower-C:
*Skis tipped uphill
Torso facing bases
(downhill)*

Transition:
*Skis tipping downhill
Torso turning uphill
Countered relationship neutral*

Lower-C

Fall line

Torso faces
outside of arc

High-C:
*Skis tipped downhill
Torso facing bases*

High-C

Transition
Zone

Figure 5-2. *Counteracting and tipping
throughout linked arcs.*

More Is Not Necessarily Better

If moving one millimeter in the right direction is good, then how about 100 millimeters? Back to Goldilocks — that might be too much. Just as a little caffeine can be helpful but a lot can be disruptive, too much counteracting may not give you the performance you want.

At first while you are learning, make sure you use photos or video as feedback. Just as with any new movement, you'll probably need to exaggerate at first to get the hang of it. Especially if you have the habit of rotating with the upper body, any movement in the new direction will feel awkward and extreme. Once you know how to exaggerate counteracting movements, you'll be able to evaluate their influence on your skis and perform them to the degree that creates the edge hold you seek.

Isolate then Integrate

Counteracting movements, like counterbalancing, should become a function of your tipping efforts. Ultimately, you'll synchronize your counteracting with your tipping. For counteracting to be functional in skiing, it must accompany tipping. If you slide with your feet flat, and don't tip the skis, then counteracting movements alone will get you nowhere. The movements of the torso are important, but their job is to support the tipping and flexing of the legs.

However, from the standpoint of learning new movements, some exercises will isolate the turning of the hips and torso. When you first practice the exercises, it's okay to focus on the newest movements that you are performing. Soon thereafter, though, perform even the simple dryland exercises in coordination with tipping the feet. This makes the practice most similar to actual skiing, and will speed up your integration of the new movements into your skiing.

Let's get on with the program of learning appropriate counteracting movements.

Dryland

Most of us don't perform counteracting movements with our hips on a daily basis, so it's normal to have limited success with them when you first try them on a ski slope. Better success is achieved if we practice the movements indoors ahead of time.

SIDEWAYS CHAIR SIT

Let's first perform a quick introduction to counteracting movements. Stand in front of an armless chair as though you are going to sit down on it. Before you sit, turn your whole body to face to one side or the other, so that your feet point 90 degrees to either side. Keeping the feet pointed to the side, turn your hips so that you can sit normally on the chair, facing forwards. The twist in your hips and lower back needed to achieve this is the counteracting movement. Still sitting with your feet pointed to the side, tip your feet on edge by lifting the side of each foot that's farther from the chair. This will aim the soles of your feet away from you. This is how the counteracting movements relate to foot tipping in skiing.

CARPETED RAMP WITH HIP-O-METER

Here is the Stationary Full Release to New Edges. You've seen it before (Figure 2-2), but the arrows in Figure 5-3 emphasize the coordination of the tipping of the feet with the counteracting turn of the torso. The overhead view in Figure 5-4 lets you see the rotational movements of the torso from a different perspective. You can see the shoulders, while the Hip-O-Meter reveals the movements of the pelvis.

In Figure 5-4, the white arrow on the carpeted ramp shows the fall line (the arrow points down the slope). My feet are pointing toward the fall line arrow, across the slope. The images of the boots show you the tipping angles of the boots in each frame.

As you look at the frames from top to bottom, my feet tip to the right, while my body turns to the left. This is counteracting.

Figure 5-3. *Stationary Full Release to New Edges, front view.*

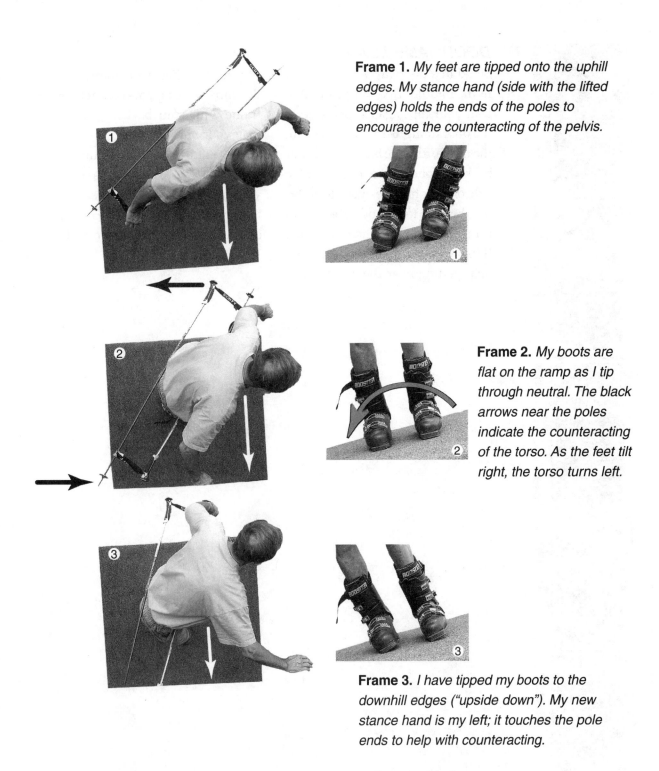

Frame 1. *My feet are tipped onto the uphill edges. My stance hand (side with the lifted edges) holds the ends of the poles to encourage the counteracting of the pelvis.*

Frame 2. *My boots are flat on the ramp as I tip through neutral. The black arrows near the poles indicate the counteracting of the torso. As the feet tilt right, the torso turns left.*

Frame 3. *I have tipped my boots to the downhill edges ("upside down"). My new stance hand is my left; it touches the pole ends to help with counteracting.*

Figure 5-4. *Stationary Full Release to New Edges, overhead and boot view.*

DOOR JAMB LEAN

Stand in a doorway with your feet in the middle. Tip your feet first to lean your hips against one side of the door frame. Before your hips hit the frame, turn the hips so that your backside touches the frame, not the side of your hip. Flex your legs and tip the feet to the other edges to bring your hips to the other side. (Push with your hands if you need help getting over there.) On your way to the other door frame, turn the hips so that you contact the frame with your backside rather than your hip.

Don't try to turn your hips so much that you land with the flat of your back on the door frame. Turn the hips enough to avoid landing on the hip bone. This may only be 10–15 degrees.

Figure 5-5. *Coordinate counteracting with tipping in a doorway.*

Tipping and Counteracting: Face the Bases

Go through the book and review the photos. In all images with the skis on edge, the torso is turned toward the stance ski. The front of the torso (the chest or the jacket zipper) faces toward the ski that is tipped onto its big-toe edge, whose little-toe edge is lifted from the snow. If you remember to always "face the base" — turn your torso to show in the same direction as the bases of the skis — you'll keep your torso synchronized with your feet.

Figure 5-6. *This is the High-C portion of the turn. The bases of the skis are lifted to show the bases to the top of the hill, so the torso also turns to face up the hill. Another way to think of this is to imagine a spectator on the hill. If the spectator can see the bottoms of the skis, she should also see the front of the torso.*

Figure 5-7. *Hopping Edge Change turns accentuate the counteracting that is necessary to land on a high edge angle. At takeoff, the ski bases and the torso face downhill. Upon landing, the skis are tipped to the new edges, with the bases showing up the hill. You can see here how the torso also turns to "face" uphill in order to maintain balance.*

Tuck Practice

Tuck turns are an ideal way to practice counteracting. The "V" formed by the poles with the hands together at the base of the V is an external cue. The feedback from the direction of the poles will help you learn to control your torso. In order for the poles to indicate the direction of the torso, the arms must squeeze the poles tightly against the sides. This ensures that the effort with the arms to aim the poles will move the torso as well. If the poles are held limply or the elbows flare out from the body, then the hands can move independently of the torso and the exercise loses its value.

STATIONARY TUCK

Review Stationary Tipping in Tuck with Counteracting, Figure 3-8.

TUCK TURNS

Squeeze the arms and poles tightly so that arms and torso behave as a unit. Point the V at the stance ski, to the side where the edges are lifting, to where the ski bases show.

Figure 5-8. *Tuck turns for counteracting practice. At transition, when the skis are flat, the hands point forward toward the ski tips. This is neutral. At the top of the new arc, the right edges of the skis are lifted from the snow, showing the bases to the right. Note that the hands point to the right, and that the entire torso has turned to face this way.*

Figure 5-9. *Tuck turns for counteracting practice. Again, pointing the poles toward the ski bases creates the desired counteracting movement. Notice here that you can see the width of the jacket front at the same time as you see the bases of the skis.*

Figure 5-10. *Tuck turns for counteracting practice. Through transition, you can see how the torso turns to point to the right as the skis are tipping to the left edges.*

Single Pole Exercises

The next exercise is fun and will challenge your counteracting movements as well as your balance. You'll make linked turns with only one pole. This exercise builds on the Hip-Touch exercise in the previous chapter, Figure 4-13.

The inside hand in each arc must press forward and upward, so that it remains at shoulder height in front of your torso. This encourages you to perform the counteracting movements with your torso. As in the counterbalancing version, the outside hand touches the hip. It can also push rearward, to encourage counteracting of the pelvis.

The turn with the pole in the inside hand is slightly easier, for two reasons. First, the out-side hand that pushes on the hip is empty, like the no-pole version, so you can push harder. Second, carrying the pole on the inside of the turn is reassuring. If you lose your balance slightly, you can drag the pole and recover.

The turn with the pole in the outside hand is slightly harder. With no pole in the inside hand, you have to work harder to maintain your balance. If you lean in slightly there will be no outrigger on which to lean. Counterbalancing movements are at a premium.

Ski a full pitch or more of turns with the pole in one hand before you switch it to the other so that you get settled into the rhythm.

Figure 5-11. *Single pole counteracting. Pole in inside hand.*

Figure 5-12. *Single pole counteracting. Pole in outside hand.*

Monitor Your Counteracting

The hips and torso play a large role in your skiing success. At turn transition, even a small movement in the wrong direction with your mid-body can detract from your tipping efforts. Unfortunately, our bodies don't give us a lot of feedback about the orientation and movements of the torso. It's important to verify your performance while you are learning so that you can reinforce the desired movements, and be aware of the incorrect ones so that you can reduce them.

Video is helpful, but it is not immediate. You will learn faster with immediate feedback from one attempt to the next. That's where the Hip-O-Meter is valuable. The poles strapped around your hips are a readout of your movements, and you can see them rather than depending on feel.

As in the previous chapter, interlock the poles using the straps around the baskets, or use small bungee cords. Make sure the hips sit on the front of your hip bones, not on your waist.

Hip-O-Meter

In Figure 4-12 in Chapter 4, Counterbalancing, the emphasis was on pushing down with the stance hand to encourage the tilt of the torso. Here, the emphasis shifts to counteracting movements. The outside or stance hand should not only press down on the poles, but also press back. The inside hand reaches high and forward, as in the Single Pole exercises.

To challenge yourself, once you have your outside hand pressing back on the poles, turn your pelvis so that you turn the Hip-O-Meter, pulling the stance end of the poles back from your hand. Touch with the hand, turn the pelvis to pull the poles back further. This shifts the emphasis of the counteracting effort to the torso, where it should be. The hand becomes a reminder of the direction of effort, rather than the motivator for moving the poles.

Figure 5-13. *Practicing counteracting with the Hip-O-Meter gives you feedback.*

The inside hand is high and forward, while the outside hand touches down and back on the pole ends. Once you touch the poles, turn your hips to pull the pole ends back away from the stance hand.

Note the carved groove from the outside (here, right) ski in the high-C arc. This is a result of tipping, counterbalancing, and counteracting.

Figure 5-14. *This demonstrates the transition of the hands as the skis tip through the edge change.*

Figure 5-15. *Harb Carvers are a perfect platform for practicing counteracting movements.*

Frame 1. *Carvers are tipped (the outside sets of wheels are off the surface) as with early, High-C tipping on snow.*

Frame 2. *Just past the fall line the inside hand is higher. The outside hand is on the pole tips as a reminder to pull the stance hip down and back. The hand lets you verify your efforts.*

Frame 3. *Coming into transition, there is still a counteracting effort. The Carvers are flattening but still on edge, so there is still a countered relationship of the torso to the legs.*

Frame 4. *In transition. The Carvers are flat on the surface, neutral, and the torso is facing forward.*

Hold the Countered Relationship Long Enough

If you start your counteracting movements in the correct direction at turn transition and continue them through the arc of the turn, all should be proceeding nicely. However, if you unwind before the next release — letting go of your counteracting efforts while the skis are still on the old edges — you will rotate the hips, lose edge grip, and lose all the energy from the arc that would have created an energetic release.

Despite your best efforts to maintain your counteracting efforts through the end of the arc, your pole swing and plant may be undermining you. Incorrect pole action will swing the shoulders around to face the ski tips, rather than keeping the torso facing the bases until the skis have released.

The next chapter will develop a pole swing that assists with your counteracting and counterbalancing. In the meantime, look at the following montage to see how far through the arc the counteracting efforts are performed.

Figure 5-16. *Keep the counteracting effort going until the moment of edge change.*

CHAPTER 6

Essential — The Complete Upper Body

C OUNTERBALANCING AND COUNTERACTING MOVEMENTS are presented in separate chapters, and they can be practiced separately. However, the best results in your skiing will come when you combine them. Progressive counterbalancing and counteracting will give you solid balance and engagement, and smooth, fluid transitions as you tip the skis from edge to edge, linking arcs. Once you start to apply both actions in linked turns, you'll find that they assist each other. It's much easier to counterbalance when you counteract with the hip in transition. You'll get more acute torso-to-leg angles from combined actions than you will from counterbalancing alone.

This presumes, of course, that you have developed the essentials in the sequence presented in this book, starting with tipping, then adding flexing and extending. Combined movements of the torso, even if perfectly synchronized with each other, are of little value if the feet and legs are not tipping the skis on and off edge. Remember, when you first start to focus on your upper body, your attention to your feet and legs will be diminished, so they may not perform as well as when you focus on them. Revisit the earlier essentials to reinforce them. We always say that skiing is like a cake — the tipping, flexing, and extending activities with the feet and legs are the cake, while the counterbalancing and counteracting activities with the torso are the icing.

Balance in the High-C Arc

MORE ENERGY IN RELEASE MEANS LESS WORK FOR THE TORSO

On the subject of balancing in the High-C arc, the more energy that you bring through transition from the previous arc, the less effort you'll have to use with your torso in counteracting and counterbalancing. If you watch World Cup skiers, you'll see that they often delay counterbalancing until the pressure starts to build in the turn — when they are facing and their skis are pointing straight down the fall line. They get away with it sometimes, when they have enough speed and they get so much thrust from the previous release that they really do float through transition.

Some of the racers use more counterbalancing and counteracting and are more disciplined with them, applying them consistently in the High-C arc. Giorgio Rocca is one of these more solid counterbalancers; that's why his skiing has become so consistent. Bode Miller is often inconsistent because he leaves his counterbalancing and counteracting until the very last moment in most turns. Bode plays a dangerous game with balance, waiting until the crux of the turn to establish it. Other racers, like Rocca and Daron Rahlves, set their angles to achieve balance much earlier in the turn. If you're going to emulate a racer, you'll have more success if you choose one who balances early in the arc. A racer with all the tools always has options; a racer with missing essentials struggles.

A LESS-ENERGETIC RELEASE REQUIRES MORE WORK TO BALANCE

If you generate little energy from the previous turn, you need greater counterbalancing with the torso to balance in the High-C arc. You'll have greater success when learning the High-C arc if you deliberately counterbalance and counteract. Even if you don't achieve a high edge angle, you'll be in balance, which develops confidence.

Many skiers are hesitant to release and transition quickly (deliberately flexing or bending the stance leg to release the pressure from the stance ski), even after they learn to arc with ski bend and energy. Being confident that you will remain in balance on the new edges makes the release seem a little less risky.

In our All-Mountain and Introduction to Racing camps, we build the technique and create the situations to be aggressive with the release. Releasing quickly does not mean that you shorten the end of the arc, exit the turn headed steeply downhill, or begin flexing the stance leg while your skis are in the fall line. It does mean that you have to release while the stance ski is still loaded and bent in the arc of the turn. If you wait too long, until you traverse across the slope after the arc, the energy of the arc is lost, making transition a chore. Practice your counteracting and counterbalancing, develop confidence in your ability to balance in the High-C arc, and you'll enjoy the easier transitions.

COUNTERACTING AND COUNTERBALANCING CAN RESCUE AN INADEQUATE RELEASE

Many skiers complain to me that they have difficulty achieving early edge engagement without a skid or push of the skis. If you don't release with a progressive flex of the stance leg while the ski is loaded in the arc, then you won't get a float. Without a float, there's little time to switch edges, encouraging the skid.

When you don't achieve float, you can save the High-C arc and engage the edges if you counterbalance and counteract aggressively, right away. If you are slow or halfhearted with your torso, the body leans downhill and starts to tumble. The only option then becomes to push the skis to the side. You may push or twist more or less depending on how out of balance you are, but in any case, the skid is revealed in your ski tracks. Walk back uphill and check to see whether you have two clean grooves at engagement, or a smudge.

Caroline Lalive of the U.S. Ski Team shows the Complete Upper Body: counteracting, counterbalancing, and a strong inside arm.

Combine Counterbalancing and Counteracting in Practice

Many exercises up until now combined counterbalancing and counteracting movements. Try them again focused on both actions: tilting laterally at the waist, turning the torso to face the lifted edges (the bases). For instance, try again:

Pole Lean & Slide (Figures 4-7-A & 4-7-B)
Door Jamb Lean (Figure 5-5)
Hip-O-Meter on Snow (Figures 4-11 & 5-13)

Hula Hoop Exercises

Using a hula hoop to practice your torso counteracting and counterbalancing enables awareness and correction of movement of your upper body. Like the Hip-O-Meter, the hula hoop gives you an external cue, feedback about what your hips and torso are doing. You can use the hands to encourage the torso to perform the desired movements as well as to evaluate your performance. Since you hold onto the hula hoop with both hands, it encourages your upper body to work as a unit, as do the tuck turns.

For the hula hoop to be most effective, it needs to be fastened snugly around your hips. We use an inexpensive weight-lifting belt and use duct tape to fasten the hoop to the back of the belt. Fasten the belt snugly around your hips, and the hula is now "connected" to you. You can turn the hoop, as though it were a giant steering wheel, you can aim the front of the hoop to your right or left, and you can tip the hoop by pressing down with one hand and lifting with the other. As long as your tape holds the hoop firmly to the belt, and the belt is snug around your hips, the hula hoop will communicate your intentions from your hands to your torso.

INDOOR HULA HOOP

Just as when you first used the Hip-O-Meter, it's helpful to perform some simple movements indoors, in front of a mirror, to see how to use the hoop.

Tip your feet from edge to edge and counterbalance with the torso. Push down on the hoop on the side with the lifted edges, and lift up on the other side. See if you can reach higher tipping and counterbalancing angles.

Tip your feet from side to side and counteract with the torso so that you "face the bases." Again, accentuate your torso efforts with your hands on the hula hoop, and see whether the nudge from the hands helps you increase the range of motion of the torso.

ON-SNOW HULA HOOP TURNS

When you start to make turns with the hula hoop, head for easy terrain without a lot of traffic. You want to be able to focus on the hoop until you are accustomed to it. Make some turns where you focus on counterbalancing, then make some where you focus on counteracting. Then, combine the two focuses. Your hands will be tipping the hoop and aiming the front of the hoop toward the bases, toward the lifted edges.

Figure 6-1. *Hula hoop turns on snow let you combine your counterbalancing and counteracting movements as well as evaluate your performance.*

Frames 1–6. *Front of torso, jacket zipper, and front of the hula hoop turn toward the stance ski; toward the lifted edges. Frame 1, old edges; Frame 2, neutral in transition; Frames 3–6, new edges.*

Frame 6. *Before the skis head downhill into the fall line, the inside hand (here, left) is lifted higher than the outside.*

HARB CARVER HULA HOOP TURNS

Since the Harb Carvers require strong, accurate tipping of the feet, they are an ideal platform for coordinating your upper body efforts with those tipping movements. Just as on snow, start with some turns where you focus on either counteracting or counterbalancing. Once you have practiced each action of the torso by it-self, combine the two and use the hula hoop to encourage the torso to move as you wish. It's especially important to practice the transition between turns, since this sets up the entire turn. Lift the new inside hand and move it forward while you tip to the new edges.

Figure 6-2. *Determined tipping, counteracting and counterbalancing goes on even after skiing at Harb Ski Systems' summer camp.*

Figure 6-3. *High-C edge angles with the counterbalancing angle established.*

Comparison of Sufficient and Insufficient Counterbalancing

It's easy to imagine a turn with completely incorrect movements of the torso, and see that it wouldn't work. However, the difference between "just right" and "not enough" can be very subtle. The following comparison of two turns will help you see the signs of sufficient or insufficient counterbalancing efforts with the torso.

SUFFICIENT, HIGH-C
The upper sequence in Figure 6-4 demonstrates high angles in the High-C arc, with just enough counterbalance. The complete turn is shown on the next page, Figure 6-5.

INSUFFICIENT, HIGH-C
The lower sequence in Figure 6-4 demonstrates high tipping and leg angles, but not enough counterbalancing. The stance leg is extended too soon, and there is too much weight on the inside ski. The complete turn is shown on the following page, Figure 6-6.

COMPARISON
The lines drawn on the figures are then placed side by side so that you can compare the leg, torso, and arm and shoulder angles more easily. You can see that in Frame 2, the angles are almost identical. By Frame 3, the difference is apparent. Though the leg angles are almost the same, the torso is leaned more inside — less counterbalanced — in the "insufficient" turn (the dashed line) and the outside arm is lifted slightly higher.

SUFFICIENT

Figure 6-4. *Comparison: sufficient vs. insufficient counterbalancing.*

Frame 2. *Almost identical.*

Frame 3. *No longer the same.*

———————— **Sufficient**

— — — — **Insufficient**

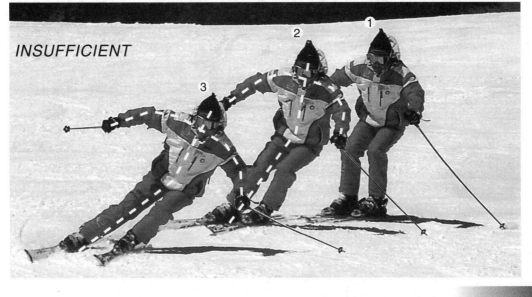

INSUFFICIENT

SUFFICIENT COUNTERBALANCING, FULL SEQUENCE

This is the same turn as shown in the comparison (with more frames shown in the upper image; frame numbering begins as in Figure 6-4). The torso-to-leg angle due to counterbalancing means I am better balanced; the increased tipping angle makes it more dynamic. The balance and energy of this turn speed up transition to the following arc and provide better float. Notice that the transition takes fewer frames here (in the lower image) than in the "insufficient" turn, Figure 6-6.

Figure 6-5. *Sufficient counterbalancing through arc results in a quick, short transition.*

INSUFFICIENT COUNTERBALANCING, FULL SEQUENCE

The turn can still be saved by flexing the legs and counterbalancing hard. I didn't actually lose my balance onto the inside ski or have to skid to recover. Flexing the legs brings the body and its center of mass closer to the feet — the base of support. Flexing and counterbalancing hard lets me tip the feet, thus the skis, to a higher edge angle, so that the turn radius will tighten bringing the skis back underneath me. The transition to the following turn takes longer, as I have less energy in the arc and am not balanced as well coming into transition as in the "sufficient" turn.

Figure 6-6. *Insufficient counterbalancing.*

Frame 6. *End of arc.*

Frame 7. *Looking for balance and pressure; not in transition yet!*

The Poles Influence the Torso's Efforts

As mentioned at the end of the last chapter, in Figure 5-16, how and when you swing your pole can influence your counterbalancing and counteracting efforts with the torso. Poles are part of the complete upper body in skiing. Correct pole use strengthens body angles and balance. Incorrect pole use can unwrap your counteracting and unfold your counterbalancing, leaving you twisting, skidding, and without grip. I've seen many skiers skiing with the right approach and technique. With everything set up, they arc toward release, but then an incorrect pole swing or plant diminishes their performance.

In this section of the book I'll demonstrate to you the pole use that assists the efforts of the torso, maintaining balance, angles, and edge grip. I'll also address adapting the pole plant to different skiing situations, from power-carving to bumps.

Both *Anyone Can Be an Expert Skier* books have extensive sections developing the mechanics of the hand, wrist, and arm in the pole swing. I'm not going to duplicate those materials here. Instead, I'm going to focus on how your pole use can support your counterbalancing and counteracting movements.

ARMS AND TORSO AS A UNIT VS. ARMS MOVE INDEPENDENTLY OF THE TORSO

In skiing, we have two ways that we use the arms. They can be made to perform as a unit with the torso, or they can perform independently of the torso.

In counterbalancing, the arm and shoulder on the stance side lean down toward the hip, tilting the torso, creating the torso-to-leg angle. In tuck turns, squeezing the arms against the sides means that pointing the hands towards the stance ski will turn the entire torso to face that way — counteracting. In both of these examples, the arms are acting as a unit with the torso.

Through the Lower-C arc, while counteracting and counterbalancing efforts hold the torso balanced and steady over the loaded stance leg, the outside hand and arm must swing the outside pole in preparation for the pole plant and transition. These arm movements must be independent of the torso. They cannot be allowed to disrupt the torso. The leg, hip, and upper body must be skeletally aligned to control the building loads of the turn. Your power for edge hold and bending the ski comes through ski and body angles, and the skeletal alignment to the skis. You can't let the pole swing pull you out of angles.

HELPFUL SWING

In a good pole swing, the hand, wrist, and forearm swing the pole at the desired time and direction, while the upper arm and shoulder help to hold the counterbalancing and counteracting angles of the torso. The forearm is independent of the torso.

DETRIMENTAL SWING

Many skiers hurt their performance by involving the torso when they swing their pole. The arm does not move independently of the torso. Instead, the pole swing draws the shoulder forward, toward the ski tip, unwrapping the counteracted relationship of the torso to the legs.

The Lower-C arc, where the pole swing must begin, and the bottom of the arc, where the pole plant must occur, have some of the highest turning loads. If your pole swing rotates your torso or lifts your outside hip even a little, your counterbalancing or counteracting angles will diminish, your ski edge angle will be reduced, your grip will be diminished, and you may skid or have the tails wash out. This is exactly the wrong moment to lose the energy of the arc and the grip and bend of the ski, since your transition to the next turn is jeopardized.

Sabine Egger of the Austrian National Ski Team demonstrates counteracting and counterbalancing movements. Notice that blocking with the outside hand has not rotated her hips or shoulders. Her left arm has moved independently of the torso in order to block.

VERSATILITY

Versatility with your pole swing means you can use any pole swing, and coordinate the poles with any type and size of turn, without the poles dictating your technique. The pole swing is often the distinguishing factor between a truly developed expert skier and a developing skier. Even skiers who demonstrate strong carving and pressuring are missing a component of the "complete game" if their pole touch is mistimed or out of sequence with the release. To the trained eye this is obvious, yet many otherwise expert skiers are unaware how changing their pole swing and timing will move their skiing to the next level.

Figure 6-7. *Counteracting and counterbalancing produce a strong, solid hip and torso, which allow the legs to flex and shorten for a powerful release. The pole basket has been swung into place for the tap without pulling the hips out of their counteracted, counterbalanced angles.*

VERSATILITY WITH THE POLES

Figure 6-8. *The pole swing and tap suitable for carving.*

In bumps and in short turns on steep terrain, the pole swing and plant will be different than in deep-angle carving turns on the groomed. In carving and turns where you're looking for round arcs and the High-C engagement, the pole plant is merely a tap; the pole is not planted aggressively into the snow. The pole basket is not swung as far forward, so the pole shaft doesn't swing far beyond vertical. Tapping the pole with the basket under the hand, rather than downhill from the hand, yields a softer touch and less impact on the torso, hence a smoother transition.

The ridge turn demonstrates a pole plant suitable for bumps. The basket is swung further forward, so there is a greater forward-pointing angle of the pole shaft prior to the plant. When the pole is planted, the basket is still downhill of the planting hand. There is a solid plant. However, compared to an aggressive blocking pole plant of 20 years ago, the new version is not as forceful. The emphasis is on creating less rebound of the pole after the plant.

Figure 6-9. *The pole swing and plant suitable for bumps and steeps.*

Figure 6-10. *After the pole tap, the planting arm and hand (here, my right) move forward, downhill — not closer to the snow — to become the new inside arm.*

Immediately after the pole tap, the planting hand and arm become the inside hand and arm for the new arc. As I explained in many of the exercises in the counterbalancing and counteracting chapters, Chapters 3 and 4, the inside arm needs to stay high and forward to support the balance and angles of the torso.

Many skiers, after the pole tap, drop the new inside hand into the "briefcase position":
arm hanging down, hand next to or below the inside hip, palm facing the leg, knuckles aimed at the ground. Letting the hand drop after the pole tap into the briefcase position is a surefire way to make your shoulders lean into the turn and to rotate the torso into the arc of the turn. It's *not* the way to strong balance and edge angles.

Figure 6-11. *Swing the outside pole into position for the pole tap without lifting or advancing the shoulder. Swing the basket straight down the fall line, not along the arc of your turn.*

Frames 1–2. *Coming through neutral, the hands are level.*
Frames 3–4. *Before the skis are in the fall line, the outside hand is starting to swing the pole basket forward, down the fall line.*

Frames 5–6. *The pole swings to bring the tip into position for the tap. The action of swinging the pole has actually enhanced the counterbalancing and counteracting movements of the torso.*
Frame 7. *Tap the pole and move that hand forward, keeping up with your speed of travel.*

HOLDING THE POLES

Home Base is where you normally hold your arms and poles while skiing. The hands should be at least 12 inches away from the body, out to the sides. You want some muscle tension through the arms to maintain Home Base, but not so much that you cannot swing the poles fluidly. Hold the poles firmly with all fingers grasping the handle. Mistakes in pole swing can arise from a loose grip.

Figure 6-12. *A strong Home Base keeps the shoulders acting in unison with the torso, and can help prevent the reaching pole swing that pulls your body out of its angles.*

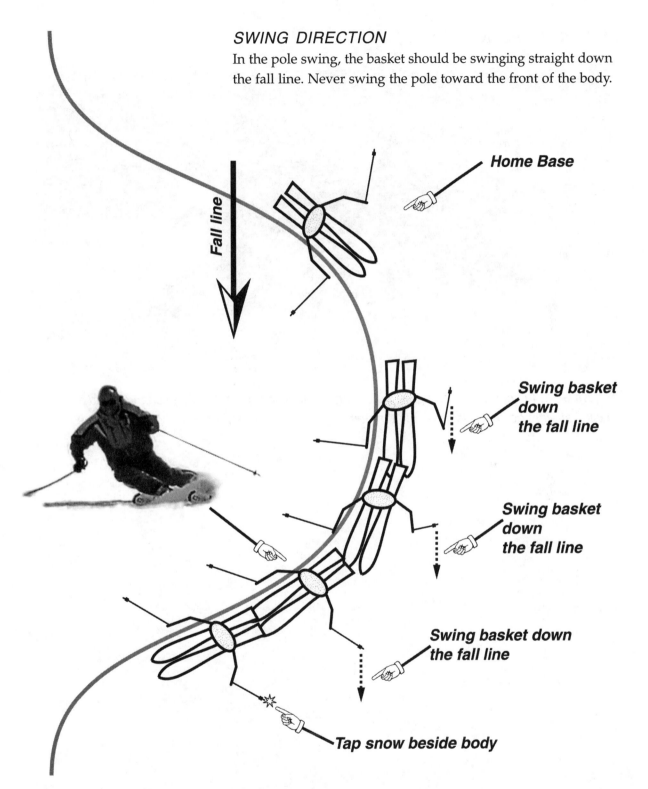

SWING DIRECTION
In the pole swing, the basket should be swinging straight down the fall line. Never swing the pole toward the front of the body.

Fall line

Home Base

Swing basket down the fall line

Swing basket down the fall line

Swing basket down the fall line

Tap snow beside body

Figure 6-13. *Pole swing diagram: Swing the basket straight down the fall line.*

Figure 6-14. *In short turns, swing the pole early, beginning right at the edge change, and aim the basket straight down the fall line. Tap the pole in passing and keep up with the speed of the turn.*

CHAPTER 7

Essential — Fore/Aft Balance

FORE/AFT BALANCE CAN BE ELUSIVE, creating frustration for any skier regardless of ability. Until I discovered "free foot management" — pulling the free foot back under my hips to re-center — the inconsistency of my fore/aft balance was concerning. Although I had good days and very good races, there was always the gamble that my fore/aft balance would slip into a back-seat experience from which I couldn't recover. If you don't have a strategy, a technique for adjusting your fore/aft balance, it's like flying blind. You never know when your skis will take off and leave you behind. In a ski race, there isn't time to make large adjustments to recover balance, so if you lose your balance and sit back, you usually lose big chunks of time or ski out of the course. If you're a recreational skier venturing onto steeper slopes, there's nothing like a session of holding on in the back seat to send you sheepishly back to the easier slopes.

When you finally learn that getting caught back on your skis is avoidable (or that you can at least recover from it), your confidence in all situations increases. How can you transform yourself into a skier with consistent fore/aft balance? Start by taking an inventory of your Home Base stance, and your ability to sense the indicators of fore/aft balance.

As you stand on your skis in Home Base, as though you were about to push off into a series of turns, where is the pressure under your feet? Are you standing on your heels, or on the balls of your feet? Can you sense how pressure is distributed under the soles of your feet? Do you feel pressure on your legs from the front and back of the ski boots? Are you able to flex your ankles and the boots enough to move the skis back so that your feet are behind your hips, as described in some of the upcoming exercises?

Once you have gone through the fore/aft sensing and range-of-motion checklist while stationary, evaluate any changes that take place once you start sliding. Don't assume that simply because you can stand balanced fore/aft while stationary that you'll achieve it while sliding. Many skiers change how they stand on their skis once they start moving, without being aware of it. Instinct and defense mechanisms take over.

As you practice maintaining and adjusting your fore/aft balance, start on easy terrain where you're not likely to be facing fear. If you're in terrain that truly intimidates you into the back seat, then your first attempts at the techniques in this chapter won't be sufficient to overcome that. Learn and strengthen your new movements on easier terrain before you put them to the test in challenging conditions.

Remember that fore/aft balance has to be practiced, just like tipping or counterbalancing. It's an essential, and you have to practice it in progressively more difficult exercises to integrate it into your skiing.

Figure 7-1. *Here is an exaggerated example of the transition that bring the hips forward and back over the boots. The upper body bends at the waist to bring the shoulders over the boots. As the legs flex, the feet can be held back, which moves the hips into position over the boots.*

Sensing Fore/Aft Balance

To analyze and improve our fore/aft balance, we have to contemplate how we judge our balance, and how we can adjust it. In tangible terms, fore/aft balance has to do with the position of our body (center of mass) relative to our feet (base of support).

First, how do we determine or sense where our body is relative to our feet? Most of us don't have very good spatial awareness of the position and location of our torso. By the time we sense that our hips are too far back, we're in really big trouble: 1. They have to be far out of place before we sense it; 2. The hips and the rest of the torso constitute a large portion of our body, so when they're far out of place it's going to take a large effort to get them back where we want them.

Where else can we sense our fore/aft balance, if not within the torso? In our feet and lower legs! If you begin to focus on the sensation of pressure on the soles of the feet, or contact with the ski boot cuff on the front and back of the lower leg (shin and calf), you will have immediate feedback about fore/aft balance. If your balance is forward, you'll feel more pressure under the ball of the foot; if your balance is back, you'll feel more pressure under (or heavier on) the heel. Similarly, if your balance is forward you'll feel more pressure from the boot cuff on your shin; if your balance is back, you'll feel more pressure on your calf. Both the feet and legs are much better areas than the hips for sensing and for feedback. By focusing on these areas, you'll receive feedback about small changes in your balance.

Figure 7-2. *This montage demonstrates the transition of the hips from inside and low in the previous turn to up and over the boots in the early part of the new turn. How is this accomplished?*

Adjusting Balance with the Feet, Not the Torso

Second, now that we have a good way to judge our fore/aft balance — a good source of feedback — what parts of our body shall we move if we need to adjust that balance? If having our balance too far back means that our hips are too far back, then shouldn't we just move the hips forward to fix the problem? I'm sure that many readers have heard the phrase, "Get your hips forward," perhaps even addressed to you. Though this might seem logical, trying to move the hips forward is not your best plan.

Remember that we're trying to adjust the location of the hips *relative to the feet*. There are two ways to achieve this: 1. Move the hips forward; 2. Move the feet back. In order to move the hips forward, we need to push or lever off of something solid — in this case, the ground. The only part of us in contact with the ground is our feet, so that hints toward option two. Second, even if we were able to move the torso without influence of the feet, it's the biggest part of us — moving it takes a lot of effort. Third, once you get it going, it's going to take an effort to stop it in "the right place," and you might even overshoot.

Let's look at option two, moving the feet back. Since the feet (even with boots and skis) are lighter than your torso, it's easier to move them relative to your body. It takes less effort to get them going in the desired direction, and once they are going, it's easier to stop them. There's another important benefit of moving the feet to adjust fore/aft balance. As you move the feet, you receive immediate feedback in the feet and lower legs. This lets you fine-tune your balancing efforts, not only through better sensing of balance, but through more finesse in making the adjustment movements.

Figure 7-3. *This is a classic Super Phantom transition. In Frame 2, my stance pressure is on the little-toe, uphill edge. My old stance leg is flexed and light. Given this situation I can flex and pull the foot back or at least hold it from moving forward.*

Fore/Aft Balance: Process or Position

Now that we have a good way to sense and to adjust our fore/aft balance, we have to consider the concept itself. If you think correct fore/aft balance is a position, then you will be apprehensive of moving your skis forward and backward underneath you. You will almost always be out of balance because you will be unable to react to changes in balance that are needed as a result of the terrain or a turn.

Instead, maintaining fore/aft balance is a process. Sometimes you will need to react to changes in your balance that you didn't foresee; other times you will be able to adjust your fore/aft balance to precede a need. In this process of balancing, you'll be moving the feet slightly forward and rearward under your hips. If you need to be more forward, pull the feet back. If you need your balance to be further aft, stand with pressure just behind your arch and your skis will move slightly forward. It's important to note that this does not imply "push your feet forward." Letting the feet move forward occurs by standing in balance at the back of the arch. Through the arc of a turn, the skis will tend to move forward in a controlled manner. There is no effort to push them forward.

Most skiers fear and have difficulty letting the feet move forward. I think this is because once skiers "get back," they don't know how to re-center quickly enough for the next turn. It is this missing essential that makes skiers stiff, static, and often fearful of trying new terrain and movements. In addition, missing this es-sential leaves them prone to losing control. Though the effort to pull one or both feet back can be applied anywhere, it is most effective when applied in transition. The best time to pull the feet back, and thus bring the hips over the feet, is just at release, between arcs, when the skis are flat on the snow and lightly pressured. This is the "float" that I described in Chapter 3, Flexing and Extending. Expert skiers do this, and it's part of what makes them excel.

Practice: Way-Forward Exercises

This first series of exercises will help you learn to pull your feet back in unison until they are behind your hips. Not only will you learn the movements of pulling the feet back, you'll also become accustomed to standing differently. If you've never had your hips ahead of your feet while skiing, you might feel that you are hanging over the tips of your skis.

Fore/aft balance is a spectrum, from back, through centered, to forward. Most skiers have spent the majority of their skiing time in the part of the spectrum from center to back, with occasional, uncomfortable excursions to "way-back." You have to know what forward is like, and how to reach it, in order to maintain fore/aft balance with more consistency. These "way-forward" exercises introduce you to the other side of the spectrum. We use them at our camps with good results. Repeated practice will help you react to fore/aft balance needs in all skiing situations.

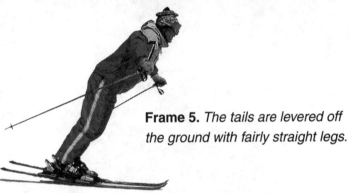

Frame 5. *The tails are levered off the ground with fairly straight legs.*

Figure 7-4. *While standing on very gentle terrain, pull the feet back until they lever the ski tails off the snow, then lower the tails. The skis may start to slide forward during the exercise. This is okay.*

PULL BACK BOTH HEELS

On a flat area or very gentle hill, pull both feet back at once until you lever the ski tails off the snow. You might need to lean slightly forward with the shoulders to get started. It's important to differentiate between hopping the tails off the ground, and levering them. One can bend the legs quickly and hop the tails off the snow, but this will not force you into the way-forward range of balance. Instead, pull the feet so far back that the skis bend in front of your bindings. Note in Frame 5 that the tails are lifted, but the legs are fairly straight.

TUCK PULLBACK

Here, Jay holds my head to demonstrate that the feet move aft relative to the hips. The torso stays in place. Stand on a flat area in a tuck, and have a friend hold your head. Pull both of your feet back until the body extends and the feet are well behind the hips. Aim for a smooth pullback, not jerky. Your friend should prevent you from moving your head forward.

Some skiers find the sensation of the skis moving backward underneath the hips disconcerting. This movement needs to become part of your skiing repertoire, as it's a key to maintaining fore/aft balance.

Figure 7-5-A. *Pull both feet back in a tuck.*

Starting Tuck | *Pullback*

Figure 7-5-B. *Pull both feet back in a tuck.*

SLIDING HEEL PULLBACKS

The next step is to perform several heel pull-backs, like the single version, while sliding. Head downhill on a very gentle slope. Pull both feet back at once until the tails lever off the snow, then slowly let the feet slide back under your hips. Keep sliding, and repeat the pull-back.

Figure 7-6. *While sliding on very gentle terrain, pull the feet back until they lever the ski tails off the snow, then lower the tails; repeat several times.*

Pullback with Ski Tipping

Now that you can pull both feet back so that your hips are way ahead of your feet, it's time to add some tipping actions and make some turns. These are not smooth, refined arcs. We're still in exercise mode here, combining some of the tipping you learned back in Chapter 2, Tipping, with the foot pullback and way-forward balance. The idea is to make some turns, starting each arc with your balance way-forward, as the first step toward integrating fore/aft balance management into your skiing.

If you've always skied with your balance behind center — with your feet ahead of your hips — you'll probably find these exercises quite strenuous. Each time that you are heaving your feet back, you're making a large shift in balance. Stick with the practice. This can be the biggest change you'll make in your skiing, making the rest of the essentials come more easily.

Figure 7-7. *Slide on a gentle slope, and pull both heels back until the tails lift from the ground. At this moment, tip both skis to one side. As the tails come back down to the snow, try to land on your edges. Balance on them for a moment, then pull the feet back until the tails lift and tip the feet to the other edges.*

Figure 7-8. *The same exercise with a more exaggerated pullback. The goal is not to pivot the skis on the tips, but rather to tip the skis on edge with your balance far forward. The inset photo is to show that both tails are levered off the snow together (not visible in the main montage).*

Building Fore/Aft Awareness and Ability

One of the fundamental principles in PMTS technique is controlling balance with the free foot. The previous exercises worked on a two-footed pullback. By working with both feet at once, the action of pulling the feet back has to be stronger. As well, having both feet back behind the hips ensures that you gain familiarity with way-forward balance. Using a single-footed pullback with just the free foot is more refined, has more finesse, and is closer to what you'll learn to use regularly in your skiing. However, if your balance is consistently too far back, then the free-foot pullback may not be sufficient to get you to a more centered Home Base in your skiing.

The next exercises emphasize one-footed balance, and using the free foot to modulate your balance. Teetering the free ski (tipping it fore/aft) will make you aware of the influence of the free ski on your fore/aft balance, and develop your ability to manage that foot to maintain or change your fore/aft balance.

To teeter the skis, combine two efforts: tipping the lifted foot toe-up and toe-down, and moving the free foot forward and rearward. To touch the ski tip to the snow, pull the free foot back and aim the toes down. To touch the tail to the snow, swing the free foot forward and lift the toes up. Use subtle movements, as little input as needed to touch the end of the ski to the snow.

Caroline Lalive of the U.S. Ski Team maintains forward pressure on the stance ski by lifting the tail of the free ski.

Figure 7-9. *Traverse on a moderate slope and lift the uphill ski off the snow. Teeter the free ski tip-up and tip-down several times as you traverse. Practice enough to become comfortable with one-footed balance. Notice the change in the upper body and hip relationship as you switch from tip-up to tip-down, and vice-versa.*

Figure 7-10. *Same exercise, side view. Notice that the transition from tip-up to tip-down is smooth and gradual, with the body balanced throughout. Look at the position of the stance foot relative to the hips in the tip-up and tip-down positions. The differences are due to the fore/aft movements of the free foot. When the free foot swings forward (tip-up), the balance is aft; when the free foot is pulled back (tip-down), the hips stay forward over the stance foot.*

TEETERING FREE FOOT IN TURNS

In this next exercise, we take the fore/aft movements of the free foot and put them into linked turns. Start on a gentle, open slope. Make some turns where you lift the free (inside) ski off the snow for as much of the arc as possible. If you can perform a Super Phantom transition (balance on the little-toe edge of the new stance ski before you tip the new free ski), that's best. Once you can make a series of turns with the free ski lifted, then teeter that ski tip-up, tip-down, several times throughout the arc of the turn. Again, be aware of changes in your balance due to the movements of the free foot.

Figure 7-11. *Teeter the free foot throughout the turn to experiment with its influence on your fore/ aft balance.*

ONE-FOOTED BALANCE, DRYLAND

These one-footed exercises challenge not only your fore/aft balance, but your lateral balancing ability as well. Here are several dryland exercises you can do to challenge and improve your one-footed balance.

Figure 7-12-A. *Roll your stance foot to the big-toe edge; balance on it.*

Figure 7-12-B. *Roll your stance foot to the little-toe edge; balance on it.*

Figure 7-12-C. *Stand on an old pole or wooden dowel; balance on it without tilting off.*

Javelin Arcs

The Javelin Arcs that I present here will challenge your balance, lateral and fore/aft. They are not easy, but they will get you forward on your skis. Even advanced skiers will learn and improve with these exercises.

If you are familiar with traditional javelin turns, you'll notice that the emphasis here is on fore/aft balance, not on achieving the extreme countering angles of traditional javelins. For these exercises, lift the inside ski, and hold the tip of the free ski over the tip of the stance ski, as though they were stacked vertically. Only the first few inches of the tips can cross. Pull the lifted free foot back until the free boot hovers just above the stance boot.

The free foot needs to tip the free ski as well as pulling back. Notice that the free leg is flexed or bent — the thigh is almost level with the snow through the Lower-C arc. This exercise combines several of the essentials.

Figure 7-13. *At the beginning of this sequence, a strong pullback is required. Maintain the stacked free ski throughout the turn, then set it down and switch at transition. Balance on the stance foot is as important as being able to move forward.*

Figure 7-14. *The effort to pull back the free ski, and keep its tip over the stance ski tip, will keep your hips forward.*

Fore/Aft Balance in Skiing

Through the exercises in this chapter, you should have an improved awareness of your fore/aft balance and the movements to adjust that balance, whether a large recovery or a fine adjustment. Do you have a plan for maintaining your fore/aft balance over long stretches of linked turns? How about a plan for those special locations that seem to send you to the back seat: moguls, transitions to steeper pitches, icy patches?

Since it's easiest to pull one or both skis back when they are flat and/or light, then the turn transition becomes the likeliest location to make these balance adjustments. Both skis are flat in transition; the slippery bases offer little resistance to being pulled back. When the free foot is less pressured than the stance foot, or perhaps lifted, it, too, can easily be pulled back.

Make a series of turns on gentle terrain where in each transition, when the skis are flat, you pull them both back. You don't have to pull so far back that the tails lever off the snow, as in the way-forward exercises, but pull them far enough back that your boots are behind your hips. If you aren't sure how far this is, use video to confirm your performance. With practice, you should be able to make these turns look smooth and almost effortless, so that an observer would wonder how you were getting your hips so far ahead to start each turn!

Make another series of turns where, in transition, you pull the free foot back so that it is even fore/aft with the stance boot. Again, you should practice this movement in linked arcs until the movement is almost undetectable, though the results will be visible.

Take these series of turns to more challenging terrain, and keep going with the pullback in every transition. Soon, you'll learn where you need to pull both feet back, and where you need to pull the free foot back, to maintain fore/aft balance in your comfort range.

closing thoughts

THE SKI INDUSTRY IS HEALTHY AND IN GOOD SHAPE, as substantiated by the growth and improvements in individual resorts. Although new resorts are not starting at the rates we saw in the 1980s and 1990s, growth is coming from within established ski resorts. New terrain is being added and lift capacity is increasing.

Besides real estate, the other focus in the ski industry is snowmaking. Snowmaking has become a prerequisite for resort operation, as seasonal changes interfere with both early and mid-season snowfalls. Consistent conditions throughout the season are a must if high-overhead mega-resorts are to balance their budgets. Regional operators nationwide are adjusting to individual problems based on climate variability, facing the daunting problems of midwinter rain and accompanying skier apathy. Altitude is becoming a real asset, enabling early and long seasons.

More than any other region, Colorado has the answer to providing a six to seven-month ski season. Cold, dry air makes for snowmaking efficiency, and this is what Colorado has above 12,000 feet, starting in September and October, even before the natural snows arrive. There is no lack of enthusiasm for the early resort openings in Colorado. Resorts race each other to be the first in the nation to open, and skiers line up to get a jump on the rest of the country.

Local enthusiasts may only be an hour's drive from these conditions, but racers come from around the world to begin on-snow training for the upcoming season. Every October and November, you can see the world's best skiers in Colorado, training on snow that was delivered to the slopes via the snowmaking system. Colorado's early season is a benefit to the industry and to the racers who come here to train.

There are more ski racers than ever, with more and more of them participating in the sport year-round. More training resorts in the southern hemisphere develop every year, responding to the demand from North American and European racers alike for year-round "winter" snow.

So, though changes in the climate are here and are influencing our sport, in the short-term we are finding plenty of solutions for skiing mileage.

What's Happening in Ski Instruction?

Skier numbers are steady but not increasing. The number of skiers taking lessons, or returning for more lessons, has not increased. Recent industry studies show that only 1.5 out of 10 skiers who take a beginner lesson turn into regular skiers. This number has been essentially the same since before I wrote my first book. Evidently, the ski industry must think that it's better to do what you've always done and hope that this number doesn't slip down to one in ten, rather than try a different approach in hopes of making it grow to two (or more) out of ten.

Ski Area Management magazine recently published an article on developments in ski teaching. The article showed that little or nothing different is happening in ski instruction, except the minor revolution started by PMTS Direct Parallel, Harb Ski Systems, and my first book, *Anyone Can Be an Expert Skier 1*. Solvista Basin (formerly Silver Creek Resort) in Colorado, a convert to PMTS Direct Parallel, showed that customer satisfaction tripled after they switched to PMTS Direct Parallel. As happened the last time that *Ski Area Management* wrote an article espousing the benefits of PMTS, they have received no questions about the program, no feedback about the article, from the industry — none. The message is, traditional instruction is the norm, it's achieving about the same results as it did ten years ago, and the industry is satisfied with that.

As far as I can see in observing traditional lessons, observing skiers, and listening to our camp participants, there is very little new in most ski instruction. Every so often, I hear an instructor telling a student to tip their skis, or perhaps to start a turn by lifting and tipping. That is more than I expected and it brings me some satisfaction, but lift and tip without the complete package doesn't produce the results that it could, and can only keep the students' interest for so long.

Even since, or despite, the introduction of shaped skis, traditional instruction has been using the same material as always for teaching skiers to get down the hill. The industry has not stepped up and demanded anything different, and ski instruction as a whole is not providing it. So why is it that PMTS technique keeps evolving and staying fresh?

Refinements in PMTS Direct Parallel

Harb Ski Systems is driven to help skiers enjoy and improve at skiing, to reach the performance they desire. If a skier is motivated to become the best she or he can be, we can do it, and do it quickly. We do that through instruction, as well as through equipment selection and tailoring at our ski shop. We work with the instructors who teach PMTS Direct Parallel to their students as well as with our own students.

PMTS Direct Parallel teaches the movements of expert skiing to all skiers. It's not just a program for beginners, and it's not just a program for already-advanced skiers. The exercises and learning situations that develop and refine a skier's movement capability will be different for the novice than for the racer, but the underlying movements being practiced are the same. By learning the right material from the start, and practicing the relevant movements each time you ski, progress toward top-level skiing is faster and more direct.

For any skier who wants to progress and become the best skier they can be, PMTS Direct Parallel enables this. How far a skier progresses, and how quickly, depends on the skier's motivation, time, athletic ability, and enjoyment of excitement. If you want a quick tune-up without getting too technical, a few practice sessions with exercises from *Harald Harb's Essentials of Skiing* will make a noticeable improvement. If you want to take your performance to the highest level, we can take you there.

Because we work with so many skiers, from novices through racers, we observe how they learn, which movements are more challenging to learn, which concepts are harder to grasp. We can observe to a certain degree what skiers have been able to learn on their own from my previous books. When we notice difficulties or stumbling blocks, we can react to try to improve the rate at which students can surmount those challenges. Sometimes the upgrades are in wording or explanation of a concept; other times I'll notice that a new exercise seems particularly effective at producing a desired movement change for numerous skiers. Immediate upgrades appear on our web site,

in the PMTS.org newsletter, and in Harald's postings on the PMTS internet forum. Major productions, such as books and videos, appear every few years.

Though the underlying movements and concepts of PMTS Direct Parallel have not changed since I presented it in *Anyone Can Be an Expert Skier 1* (and indeed, since I coached with those movements in the 1970s), there have been changes in emphasis and presentation. The ski teaching system, in all its presentations, has adapted to optimize the results of our students. I don't have to answer to a large organization. I answer to the needs of my customers, students, readers, and viewers, and to their motivation for skiing enjoyment. If something doesn't work, I change it. If some aspect of our teaching system can be better, I improve it. I don't understand the mindset of repeating past errors and turning off new generations of skiers.

Pieces of a Puzzle

In this new book, *Harald Harb's Essentials of Skiing*, there are some catchy new approaches as well as solid, tried-and-true approaches that I have used for decades in the business of developing elite athletes. You may well see exercises here that you've seen before, either in my materials, or elsewhere.

The organization of this book is like a puzzle within a puzzle. The exercises are not a jumble of material lumped together, or diluted with inconsistencies. The exercises within one chapter fit together to improve that movement or essential. The essentials fit and work with each other to produce top skiing performance.

Results Lead to Commitment to Learning

The exercises in this book should produce tangible results for you in a short time. This should help you to trust the material and what you are learning. Confidence and trust promote motivation and belief in the outcome.

When you are learning, if you know what you are learning and you know that it is what you want or need to learn, then you are much more likely to commit yourself to that program. A skier committed to PMTS technique is a highly energized skier. This book offers simple approaches that are immediately effective. It's a lean, mean, ski instruction book, full of what works, and trimmed of all that doesn't immediately help you to learn and improve. That's why it's called "The Essentials."

What About Skiing in Variable and All-Mountain Conditions?

Readers of *Anyone Can Be an Expert Skier 2* often missed the point that skiing all-mountain, ungroomed conditions, like powder, bumps, and crud, is not a matter of beating yourself up in those conditions until you miraculously "get it," nor is it a matter of performing 38 different "tips" specific to those conditions. The answer in that book, and now, is that you have to develop the bulletproof short turn in order to succeed and enjoy ungroomed conditions. There is no magic pill to transform movements that cause skidding on steeps and ice into movements that suddenly become effective in ungroomed snow. Back in Chapter 4, Counter-balancing, I mentioned that many skiers tell me regarding groomed slopes that, "I can ski fine up here, but when it gets steep or icy I can't control my speed." There's no reason to think that the same technique which is inadequate on steeps and ice will prove to be your ally in moguls or crud.

The movements that you need to carve on steep, icy slopes, or to link turns in control in moguls are the essentials. I understand that one can ski on groomed blue terrain without the essentials. If your goal is to ski more challenging conditions, then you need to master the essentials, and you need to practice them on all the slopes that you ski. The essentials need to *be* your technique, not just an adjunct that you bring with you to the tougher slopes.

Let me use an analogy to explain this. Skiing without the essentials is like living in Denver and not putting on snow tires for the winter. "I don't need snow tires down here, since the roads are dry 90% of the time. But driving up to the mountains is a nightmare! I'd like to go skiing, but I know my tires don't work well up there when it snows!" If you want to drive safely in the mountains, you have to have snow tires, and you have to have them on for all your winter driving. If you want to ski on the steeps, the ice, the bumps, and the powder, you have to have the essentials. If you use the essentials in all your skiing, when you venture into the more difficult conditions, your technique will work fine for you. You won't need dozens of bump or powder lessons.